Ecological Perspectives Cookbook

RECIPES FOR SOCIAL WORKERS

Ecological Perspectives Cookbook

RECIPES FOR SOCIAL WORKERS

Bruce D. Friedman

Brooks/Cole Publishing Company

I⟨T⟩P® An International Thomson Publishing Company

Pacific Grove ■ Albany ■ Belmont ■ Bonn ■ Boston
Cincinnati ■ Detroit ■ Johannesburg ■ London ■ Madrid
Melbourne ■ Mexico City ■ New York ■ Paris ■ Singapore
Tokyo ■ Toronto ■ Washington

Acquisitions Editor: *Lisa I. Gebo*
Marketing Team: *Steve Catalano,*
  Jean Thompson, Aaron Eden
Editorial Assistant: *Susan Wilson*
Production Editor: *Mary Vezilich*
Production Service: *Anne Draus,*
  Scratchgravel Publishing Services

Permissions Editor: *May Clark*
Manuscript Editor: *Betty Berenson*
Cover Design: *Vernon T. Boes*
Cover Art: *Harry Briggs*
Typesetting: *Scratchgravel Publishing Services*
Printing and Binding: *Webcom*

For more information, contact:

BROOKS/COLE PUBLISHING COMPANY
511 Forest Lodge Road
Pacific Grove, CA 93950
USA

International Thomson Editores
Seneca 53
Col. Polanco
115060 México, D. F., México

International Thomson Publishing Europe
Berkshire House 168-173
High Holborn
London WC1V 7AA
England

International Thomson Publishing GmbH
Königswinterer Strasse 418
53227 Bonn
Germany

International Thomson Publishing Asia
60 Albert Street
#15-01 Albert Complex
Singapore 189969

Thomas Nelson Australia
102 Dodds Street
South Melbourne, 3205
Victoria, Australia

Nelson Canada
1120 Birchmount Road
Scarborough, Ontario
Canada M1K 5G4

International Thomson Publishing Japan
Hirakawacho Kyowa Building, 3F
2-2-1 Hirakawacho
Chiyoda-ku, Tokyo 102
Japan

Printed in Canada

10   9   8   7   6   5   4   3   2   1

Library of Congress Cataloging-in-Publication Data

Friedman, Bruce D., [date]–
    Ecological perspectives cookbook : recipes for social workers /
Bruce D. Friedman.
        p.   cm.
    Includes bibliographical references and index.
    ISBN 0-534-34410-0 (alk. paper)
    1. Social service.   I. Title.
HV41.F685   1999
361.3'2—dc21   98-30208
                                                CIP

Dedicated to simplifying our lives—
with the help of metaphors

CONTENTS

PREFACE

The social work profession is quite complex. As a profession, social work's primary mission is to enhance human well-being and help meet the basic human needs of all people (NASW, 1996, p. 1). However, how to do this is not clearly defined. The profession draws on different complex and profound concepts to explain the "how to."

As social work educators it becomes our role to explain these complex and profound concepts (mostly borrowed from other disciplines) and present them to students in a manner in which they can be applied to the work of the profession. The use of metaphor is one way to do this. Metaphors provide common reference points and can diffuse anxiety from the concept. For me, food is such a useful metaphor. You, of course, probably have your own metaphors to explain complex concepts. This book is not intended to limit your use of metaphors but rather to provide a tool to assist you in helping students understand social work concepts through the use of metaphors.

While this cookbook is meant to be fun, it is not just humor and a few good recipes that are presented. Rather, this cookbook is a supplemental text intended to illuminate—albeit in an unusual way—the core concepts of the social work profession and social work education.

I invite readers to build on concepts by creating your own metaphors at the end of each chapter. Whether your interest is gardening, sports, mechanics, art, literature, and/or the world of work, I encourage you, through critical thinking prompts, to apply your interests to the core issues in social work.

I hope you enjoy this cookbook. Try using it as a springboard to create your own personal journal as you continue your studies in social work. Feel free to share your ideas with friends, colleagues, mentors, and others. You may also find it useful to share some of your metaphors with client systems as a way to help them understand these complex concepts.

I would like to thank the following reviewers for their helpful comments: Eddie Davis, Buffalo State College; John Nasuti, University of North Carolina, Wilmington; Katherine Shank, Miami University; Barbara Thomlison, University of Calgary; and José B. Torres, University of Wisconsin–Milwaukee.

Throughout my career, I have been blessed by the people with whom I've worked. Some faculty members at Wayne State University School of Social Work and the Social Work Department at Southern Connecticut University enhanced my environment to a point where I was able to freely and openly express these ideas. I also want to thank my students who put up with me in the kitchen and sampled some of the recipes that appear in this book. I'd also like to thank Lisa Gebo, acquisitions editor with Brooks/Cole•Wadsworth, for reviewing and considering this text for publication. My sons, Jaron and Bryan, influenced my early cooking development and helped me learn how to keep things at a simple level in order to explain things clearly. Finally, I want to thank Hylla. Prior to meeting her I was only a good cook; however, through the love, encouragement, and proper seasoning techniques that she gave me, I have become a better cook. She encouraged me to explore my inner self so that I could use the food I prepare as a source of love and not just a means of sustenance. As a result, not only am I a better cook, but I also became a better social worker and person. I am forever indebted to her and the lessons that I have learned from her.

Bruce D. Friedman

CHAPTER 1

Introduction

WHAT'S IN THIS CHAPTER:

- An orientation to social work and social work education

- A discussion of metaphors as learning tools

- An overview of the ecological systems perspective

- A discussion of the scientific process versus the art of social work practice

Why a Cookbook?

There are two areas of life that are important to me—people and food. I became a social worker because of my interest in helping people, and I see food as an important component in bringing people together. People are more likely to seek help from friends before ever seeking help from a professional. Maybe that is why more helping takes place around a kitchen table than happens in agency offices. But, of course, the helping that happens around the kitchen table is not called social work.

A major difference between what happens around a kitchen table and what happens in an agency office is that the helping in the agency office is done by a social worker. That is, social workers perform a professional form of helping. "Professional helping is different from natural helping in that it is a disciplined approach focused on the needs of the clients and it requires specific knowledge, values, and skills to guide the helping activity (Morales & Sheafor, 1998, p. 28). The desire to help people led to your becoming a professional social worker. Most people agree to five basic attributes of a profession:

1. Possession of a unique skill valued by society
2. Expectation of specialized training for practitioners
3. Possession of a systematic theoretical knowledge base on which training is based
4. Existence of a code of ethics to guide practice
5. A professional organization that protects the interests of its members (Popple & Leighninger, 1996, p. 54)

People become professional social workers through education and training that involves learning complex theories and concepts about helping people. However, as a social work educator, I constantly struggle with how to take complex concepts that relate to the technical aspects of the field and translate them into common language. For me, the simplest way to explain these concepts is through the use of metaphors and more specifically by using food analogies. Since everyone has to eat to survive, food is a universal language that everyone understands. Of course, there are differences in how food is perceived by different cultures, but food still brings people together. So I see food as an aspect of helping people. Recipes are the tools to create the food that brings people together and the food is the sustenance of life. Even people who do not know how to cook can understand the basic components of a recipe and how those components are combined to produce a result. Food analogies can thus be important tools for explaining complex issues of social work and, more important, human interactions.

I decided to take these analogies and some very special recipes and present them together in a cookbook. My goal is that this will be a fun book. That is, I want this book to provide some basic information and knowledge about human interactions and also to be practical. Regardless of how knowledgeable you are of concepts, if you cannot apply the concepts to practice, they are useless. Metaphors provide a framework to help you understand concepts. My comparison is food; however, this text is not intended to limit you to that interest. If you have other interests, feel free to use them to provide greater insight into the concepts for yourself. But still, use this book to learn about social work concepts and to provide you with sustenance.

Organization of the Book

The organizing principle in social work is the *ecological systems perspective* or ecosystem. Here, an *ecosystem* model describes a stepwise theoretical model where a variety of inputs enter the system (the unit of analysis), and interactions take place within the system (intervention), resulting in an output. These take place within an ecological environment (the definition of "ecological environment" will come later). Each system operates with a feedback loop that evaluates whether the actual output matches the expected outcome. If not, then information is used to change the inputs so that the actual output will more closely match the expected outcome. Now if you can understand that, there is no need to continue with this book. That is the technical jargon. However, the jargon needs to be simplified to be understandable and effective. I hope the following descriptions and recipes will do the task.

Let me illuminate the ecosystems perspective by a cooking analogy. The cook gathers the ingredients (inputs), mixes them together (interaction), and cooks them according to instructions (intervention), with the result being the product (output). The product is tasted to see if it matches the desired result. If not, then it means going back (the feedback loop) (Friedman, 1997) to the ingredients to see what needs to be changed to achieve the desired result. There are also environmental factors, such as the age of the ingredients (ecological environment), that affect the recipe. These must be taken into consideration as well.

As you can see, cooking and baking can clarify the ecosystems perspective. I have organized this book along the ecosystems framework. I use food analogies to explain social work concepts and standards. I hope this places the social work concepts in a practical and relevant environment for everyone. Since this is an introduction to the social work profession, the book also has an academic perspective. This means that the book is organized along each of the nine curricular areas that the Council on Social Work Education (CSWE) requires each accredited social work program to cover. The nine curricular areas or standards are research, human behavior in the social environment (HBSE), practice/methods, policy, field practicum, cultural diversity, populations at risk, social and economic justice, and social work values and ethics. I hope the combination of analogies, theoretical concepts, and practical applications will make the concepts of social work come alive. But even if they don't, following the recipes will provide food for thought and appetite—food for the body and the mind. So experiment and enjoy.

What Is Social Work?

Let me begin by using the theme of this book to define social work itself. Social work is a term that was applied to a profession about 100 years ago. As social workers we also use terms such as *ecological systems, casework, group work, community organizing, advocacy,* and *case management,* but these terms and concepts are challenging to understand even by people in the field. How do we explain these concepts to people who are not familiar with the field or who are interested in joining the field? We hem and haw and then use different concepts to try to explain what we do.

Although the term *social work* is widely used, many people don't understand what the profession is. Ginsberg (1998, pp. 5–6) identifies seven reasons why the profession isn't understood:

1. Social work sounds like other disciplines and may cause confusion. There is confusion between sociology and social studies, and some may associate them with social work.

2. People outside social work view social workers by what they do or where they work rather than by their profession. In other words, social workers are more likely identified by their job title rather than as a member of the social work profession.

3. Social work is not a subject that is usually taught in elementary or secondary schools.

4. Many people do not come into contact with social workers during the normal course of their lives.

5. The media do not cover social workers or social work programs as extensively as they do other fields.

6. The social work profession has not spent as much time and money as it might to educate the public about its work.

7. Social work is not always a powerful profession although it has had degrees of success in influencing laws and budgets.

The *Social Work Dictionary* responds by defining social work as "the applied science of helping people achieve an effective level of psychosocial functioning and effecting societal changes to enhance the well-being of all people" (Barker, 1995, p. 357). But note that this definition still uses concepts to explain the concept of social work. "Effective level of psychosocial functioning" and "effecting societal changes to enhance the well-being of all people" are concepts. Would you use these concepts to explain social work to your family or friends? Let's stop using concepts to explain other concepts. Let's use an analogy that most people understand to explain the concept.

One way to think about social work is as a several-course meal. When we look at a meal, we see a multifaceted assortment of foods presented in an organized and systematic way, and we know that a lot of work went into the preparation of that meal. Each course has taken planning and preparation. Because we understand the components and preparation of the courses, we appreciate the meal. This is very similar to the social work field. The components of the field are like each course in a meal. We need to understand and appreciate each component of the field to fully understand the profession of social work. And there are many components to the profession. For example, there are social workers who work with individuals, those who work with groups, and those who work with communities. Individually, they represent only part of the profession. Just as a single course can be part of a meal and sometimes the whole meal. How many times have you had only a salad for lunch? That was sufficient for your needs at that time.

However, while you may not practice all the components of social work, to understand the profession as a whole, it is important to understand each of the components that make up the profession. At the bachelor of social work (BSW) level, this is referred to as a generalist, but generalist is just another concept that needs further explanation so that we fully understand the meaning of that concept.

Generalist Practice

Generalist social work practice is a recognized model of practice and has been described (McMahon, 1994, p. 4) as containing five essential elements:

1. An ecological system perspective
2. A problem focus
3. A problem-solving process
4. A multilevel approach
5. An open selection of theories and interventions

This translates into the ability to work with systems of different sizes utilizing a variety of interventive strategies. How does that translate into simple terms that are understandable?

A way of thinking of a generalist practitioner is to think of the difference between a good cook and a gourmet chef. A good cook is trained to be able to perform all aspects of meal preparation. A good cook understands meal planning, shopping, preparation, and presentation. The cook understands the basic components of soups, salads, main courses, side dishes, and desserts. Good cooks require training to effectively produce a satisfactory dining experience. The basics must be in place before flourishes can be added.

Generalist social workers are also trained. They learn a variety of roles related to social work. They learn to be brokers, advocates, mediators, and so on. They learn to work with systems of various sizes. The generalist social worker is like a good cook. One can expect a professionally executed intervention from a generalist social worker.

The basic difference, then, between a bachelor's degree in social work and a master's degree is not in professionalism but rather in training. Where BSWs have been trained to do a little bit of everything, MSWs specialize in a specific area. There are too many areas to highlight at this time; think of the basic difference between BSWs and MSWs as the difference between a good cook and a gourmet chef.

Regardless of whether it is a BSW or an MSW performing an intervention, each performs tasks that follow a scientific process and each adapts techniques to his or her particular style. This is referred to as the "conscious use of self" within the field and opens a discussion of whether social work is art or science.

The question of art or science is the same in social work as it is in cooking. There is a science in cooking and also an element of art.

Art or Science?

One of the major questions in social work is whether it is an art or a science. On the one hand, social work is an art. The ability to assess and problem solve to change the situation to the satisfaction of the client system* certainly involves art. However, the art does not come from nowhere. There is a philosophical foundation that supports the art. That philosophical foundation is the science of social work.

Let me use a cooking analogy to explain the art or science question in social work. Before a cook begins cooking a meal, she or he sits down and thinks about what the meal should look like. That vision is part of the art of the meal. Then the science comes into play. The cook utilizes knowledge of the preparation of each item to develop a shopping list of the ingredients needed to prepare the meal. However, preparing a shopping list is a very exacting science. Every ingredient (with appropriate quantities) needs to be anticipated. A misplaced ingredient or inappropriate quantity can add unnecessary time to the meal preparation, add unnecessary expense to the meal, or even ruin the preparation altogether. Therefore, meal preparation needs to be planned very carefully and is part of the science component of the meal.

Art is involved even in the science of recipe development. The omission or addition of an ingredient can change the recipe. Good cooks know how to combine the art of changing a recipe with the science.

This balance of art and science continues throughout the meal preparation. Attention to the details of food preparation involves science, which leads to the taste of the meal. However, the best-tasting food will not be eaten if it is displayed in an unattractive manner (which is where art comes in). Have you ever seen a cake fall? It tastes perfectly good but does not look appetizing. Therefore, presentation of the meal is also very important. As another example, while I was working in a nursing home, the residents often complained about the meals. The food tasted fine but did not look appetizing. Because the food did not look good, many residents refused to even try to eat it.

Social work is the same way. A person can have the best skills and the best scientific technique but must also be able to develop

---

*Social workers deal with client systems of all sizes, including individuals, families, groups, institutions, and communities. The word *client* typically implies an individual. To make it clear that this text is referring to all sizes of client systems, the term *client system* is used throughout the book.

a relationship with the client system in order to utilize these learned helping skills. Relationship building is the art form in social work. For if any change is to take place, there needs to be a relationship between the social worker and the client system.

Thus, social work involves a blending of art and science that relies heavily on the strengths of the worker and the interaction with the client system. This is the intervention in the social work process.

To demonstrate the concept of art and science, let me introduce a generic bread recipe. I call it generic because it is a basic recipe that can be used to make a lot of different kinds of bread. It can be put in a pan to create a sandwich loaf or it can be shaped to form a baguette. So try it out and see what type of art form you can create from the basic scientific process. Remember, the recipe represents the science; the finished product represents the art.

Generic Bread Recipe

1 tsp salt

2 tbsp sugar

2 tbsp shortening

1 ½ cup water (110 degrees F if using dry yeast)

2 tsp dry yeast or ¼ oz cake yeast

4–6 cups flour (preferably bread flour)

Place first five ingredients and 2 cups of flour into a bowl. Mix for 2 minutes until all the ingredients are dissolved. Slowly add 2 more cups of flour while mixing. The dough should pull away from the sides of the bowl when it is fully mixed, or developed. If the dough does not pull away from the sides, continue to add a little more flour until the dough pulls from the sides and forms into a ball. (Atmospheric conditions affect the amount of flour needed. During hot and humid weather, more flour will be needed. This is the ecological environmental factor.) Mix the dough until it is well developed, at least 10 minutes if using a mixer or 15 minutes by hand. After mixing, cover the dough and place it in a warm, moist place. Allow the dough to rise about 1 ½ hours. Then punch the dough to remove the air bubbles, and cut it into the type of product you want.

Now comes the art of the recipe. If you want to make bread loaves, then cut the dough into two pieces, roll each into a cylinder shape, and place each loaf in a pan. If you want to make rolls, then you can make about one dozen. Or you can make one loaf and six rolls. This dough can also be used to make about three 12-inch pizza crusts or Vienna bread, French bread, Italian bread, or kaiser rolls. What you decide to make will determine the size and shape and some of the basic baking times needed. For example, Italian bread and kaiser rolls are best if they are baked with steam. Since most homes don't have steam ovens, use a plant mister to mist the dough in the oven during the first 10 minutes of baking.

Once you decide what you want to make, let the dough shapes rise for another hour. Then bake the bread in a 350-degree oven for about 25 to 30 minutes or until it has a brown top and bottom. If you tap the bottom of the bread, it will sound hollow. Rolls take a shorter time whereas loaves will take a little longer.

The Ecological Environment

Within social work it is important for the social worker to under-stand all the factors that affect the client system. For example, when an individual is having a problem, it is important to find the source of the problem. Is the source of the problem some-thing within the individual, something that evolved because of a situation within the individual's immediate family, or a result of the effects of other members in the family? Does the source of the problem arise from a conflict between the individual's values and the social structure where the individual lives? The source of the problem may be a combination of all of these elements or just one of them. It is up to the social worker to fully understand how the individual functions within the environment. This is called person-environment fit.

Again, I am using words to try to explain this concept of ecological environment and person-environment fit. Let me use another analogy from cooking to explain these concepts.

A baker needs to be very aware of the environment when preparing baked goods. For example, most recipes are written to be carried out at sea level. A few hundred feet above sea level will not have much effect on a recipe. However, when I lived in Calgary, the altitude did affect each recipe. The cooking time and temperature needed to be adjusted to accommodate the change in altitude. As a general rule of thumb, the oven temperature needs to be about 25 degrees hotter and the baking time about 10 minutes longer when you are baking at a mile above sea level.

Other factors also affect recipes. The temperature of the water is very critical in working with yeast products. The length of mixing time is also a crucial factor, as is the freshness of the products. Each and every ingredient that is to be used in a recipe is important to obtain the proper flavor and texture of the food being prepared. And all these components in cooking and baking are elements of the ecological environment. These elements are also important considerations in social work.

Another way of looking at the ecological environment is to consider the meal itself. How the table is set is very important to the success of a meal. You cannot eat soup on a plate. It's not proper to eat vegetables with only a knife. These become important considerations when setting a table and creating the proper environment for a meal. In addition, if meal time is a time for social interaction yet the television is on in the background, then focus will be divided between the television and the other dining guests. This is another aspect of the meal's environment.

The ecological environment is critical in social work practice as well. It is important for the worker to have the proper knowledge of the client system's background to fully understand all aspects of the presenting problem. These concepts will be further discussed in other chapters of this book.

Within social work education the concepts of generalist practice, problem-solving process, and ecological environment are taught through nine curricular areas. As stated earlier, these areas are research, human behavior in the social environment, practice/

methods, policy, field practicum, cultural diversity, populations at risk, social and economic justice, and social work values and ethics. The rest of this book presents concepts associated with each of these areas and uses food analogies to explain them. Each section ends with a recipe that symbolizes the analogy. You are then asked to identify your own metaphor to explain the concept. The goal is that by using such analogies you will be able to better understand the concepts relating to social work practice.

Critical Thinking Prompts

- Try to explain what a social worker does to someone who isn't a social worker.
- Now identify a metaphor that simply explains your definition of what a social worker does.
- Do you see a difference? Does the use of metaphor and analogy make explaining the concept easier?
- Now do the same thing with generalist social work practice.
- Develop an argument for whether social work is either art or science, or both.

CHAPTER 2

Research

WHAT'S IN THIS CHAPTER:

- Description of the scientific process within social work
- How to define variables
- Brief look at evaluative standards within social work

o me, research is a logical thinking process of how to address a problem. We seek to understand a problem through our own ways of understanding and thinking about human behavior. "These types of understanding include using values, intuition, past experiences, authority, and the scientific approach" (Marlowe, 1998, p. 3). The scientific approach is research.

Research helps to guide the process used to reach the final result. And we usually have certain assumptions when we undertake a research project. First is the assumption that the goal is understood. For without knowing the goal or desired outcome, we do not know the direction in which to proceed. Second is that we have all the resources we need to get to the goal. Again, we can go on a journey but if we don't have everything we need for that journey, we will fail to get where we want to go. And third, we believe there is a process that uses the available resources to reach the goal.

The basic concepts about research are stated by the Council on Social Work Education's (CSWE) Curriculum Policy Statement (CPS): "The research curriculum must provide an understanding and appreciation of a scientific, analytic approach to building knowledge for practice and for evaluating service delivery in all areas of practice. Ethical standards of scientific inquiry must be included in the research content" (Council on Social Work Education, 1994, pp. 103, 142).

Let me turn to cooking and baking as a way to try to understand this analytic approach to building knowledge. When we begin a research project, we begin with an idea. Before we begin cooking or baking we also have an idea of what we want to make. To succeed we must check the ingredients to make sure that we have everything we need to make what we've set out to make. And, finally, we follow a logical process, called a recipe, to reach our goal.

The research principles in social work are similar. First we begin with an idea, which most likely emerged from a question or problem that we are trying to resolve. Then we need to check the ingredients, or all the elements that relate to that problem. Of course, one of the differences is that in baking it is easy to distinguish the raw ingredients from the outcomes, whereas, when dealing with human behavior, it may be harder to ascertain the difference. That is why social workers rely on theoretical knowledge to help understand differences in variables (ingredients in our metaphor).

For example, in thinking about services that address the homeless problem, one would consider the homeless shelter. But what is a homeless shelter? I performed a research study to understand what happens in a homeless shelter to address the problems of homeless people. I had to go through a number of steps just to begin the process. First I had to define the terms (obtain my ingredients). I defined *homeless shelter* as an emergency, temporary residence that provides room and board for an individual for no more than ninety days. This definition clearly differentiates individual shelters from family shelters. It also clearly states the transitional nature of a shelter as opposed to a long-term residence.

The next step involved understanding what was the expected outcome of a person going to a shelter. Was the outcome that the person would obtain permanent housing? Or was the outcome just to obtain a place to stay when the person had nowhere else to go? It was important to understand the differences between these two questions in order to understand the nature of the outcome that I would be evaluating. The assumptions from the literature were that the homeless shelter would assist people in obtaining permanent housing and that the shelter was only a transitional place to stay until a more permanent place could be found.

The next step was to develop a criterion by which to judge whether shelters were successful in achieving the stated outcome. If permanent housing was the criterion, then the question arose as to whether the shelter could help the homeless person into a permanent housing location within a certain period of time or whether the shelter only established transitional housing for homeless people. This process helped to differentiate between what I was looking at and what was actually being measured.

We already learned that the ecological systems perspective is an organizing principle in social work. Social work also relies on other theories to explain specific variables. For example, if you are baking a cake 1 mile above sea level (like Denver or Calgary) and follow the recipe carefully, the cake will still not come out right. You try to understand why the cake did not come out right since you used the listed ingredients and mixed them according to the directions. So, what affected the cake? That unknown element is the altitude. Most recipes are written to work at sea level. When you live at high elevations, you need to modify the recipe in order to obtain the same outcome. That same need, to be aware of different factors, happens when working with children. We cannot perform the same intervention with children of different ages because of differing stages of development at different ages. Therefore, it is important to understand some developmental theories in addition to the ecosystems perspective.

The organizing perspective in social work for undertaking this logical process is called *systems perspective.* I use the ecosystems perspective to introduce the logic of research and then follow it with some basic recipes.

The Ecosystems Perspective

I like to classify the ecosystems perspective as a model rather than what some people call a theory. The reason I call it a model is because it is a way of organizing a thought process. The basic systems model includes a system or organism with inputs and outcomes (Friedman & Levine-Holdowsky, 1997). The inputs are the raw ingredients that go into the system. The outcome is the end product or what interacts with the environment. The entire system rests within a larger environment called the suprasystem. This concept lends itself very nicely to baking and cooking. In order to bake or cook anything there are a number of variables. For example, the end product is very different from what initially went into the system. Therefore, some interaction took place within the system in order to create the change that produced the end result. It is this interaction within the system that is the logical process that research tries to explain. This chapter contains rather simple recipes where the process is not as important as it will be later on. Future chapters will be more specific about the process.

The outcome of the system can be classified as the *dependent variable*—that is, it is a variable that is dependent on the interaction of the other (independent variables) in order to be achieved. The *independent variable(s)* are the raw ingredients that go into the system. Some type of interaction of the raw ingredients must take place to create the dependent variable. This interaction takes place within a larger environment. And in this larger environment, there are some things that can be controlled and some that cannot be controlled. For example, in baking the oven temperature and the size of the pan can be controlled. But there are other factors that also need to be taken into consideration, such as altitude, temperature, and humidity. These will also affect the outcome. Sometimes various adjustments need to be made to the recipe to address these factors. This book will not specifically address each of these environmental factors but I mention them here to make you aware that they exist.

Social work research is very similar to baking. There are ingredients that go into the system, some interaction that takes place, and then an output. There is also a feedback loop where we see whether the output matched the desired outcome. If the output is different from the expected outcome, then we need to try to understand what went wrong. There may have been a problem with the inputs (ingredients or independent variables) or there may have been a problem with the interaction within the system. If the problem is within the system, then it is important to look at factors both inside the system (conceptual problems with the interaction) and outside the system (larger suprasystem factors that influenced the interaction). This logic holds for social work as well as for baking and cooking. A general rule of thumb in looking at any research question is to define the differences between the independent variables and the dependent variables. I like to use the analogy of a cake. Your independent variables are your raw ingredients and the dependent variable is the cake. When making a cake, it is easy, of course, to determine what are the independent and the dependent variables. With some thought it is also possible to decipher the independent and dependent variables of a research question. The difference is that you are probably more familiar with a cake than you are with the research project you are considering. So take a step back and think about which factors in the research question might cause something to happen. These will be the independent variables. Try to figure out if there are factors that might influence the output in ways that you don't want and control for those factors.

In the homeless example described earlier, the two concepts are homeless people and homeless shelters. If the outcome is that homeless people become permanently housed, then the independent variables are the homeless person and the homeless shelter. Each stands on its own independently, like the raw ingredients in a cake. The dependent variable is the transformation of the homeless person from being homeless to moving into permanent housing. The dependent variable is the goal or what one hopes to achieve. Measurement of the dependent variable would be determining how long it took to find permanent housing for each individual.

Let's look at the independent, dependent, and control variables in the following recipes.

Cutout Sugar Cookies

1 tbsp cream or nondairy creamer	1 tbsp corn syrup
1 cup sugar	2 eggs
¾ cup shortening	2¾ cups flour
1 tsp salt	1 tsp vanilla
	1 tsp baking powder

These are all independent variables. You create an interaction effect by mixing the shortening, eggs, vanilla, cream or creamer, salt, sugar, and corn syrup thoroughly. Blend in the flour and baking powder. Chill at least 1 hour.

Now you consider the factors you control—the thickness of the dough you roll and the oven temperature you use. These are very important to the success of the finished product—the outcome—but do not specifically add anything to the product.

Roll the dough about ⅛- to ¼-inch thick on a lightly floured board. Cut out cookies. Place them slightly apart on an ungreased baking sheet. (For an egg wash, beat one egg well and, using a pastry brush, "paint" each cookie with the beaten egg. Dip the cookies in sugar before placing them on the baking sheet.) Bake until cookies are golden in color, about 8 to 10 minutes in a 385-degree oven. The yield—the outcome—will be four dozen cookies.

For those of you who prefer chocolate chip cookies to sugar cookies, here is an alternative recipe:

Chocolate Chip Cookies

½ cup brown sugar	1 tbsp water
½ cup granulated sugar	½ tsp baking soda (dissolve in water)
1 tsp salt	
1 tbsp cream or nondairy creamer	1 tsp vanilla
	1¼ cups flour
¾ cup shortening	¾ cup chocolate chips
2 eggs	

These, again, are the independent variables. You mix them thoroughly for the interaction effect. (There is no need to refrigerate this dough.) Then drop the dough onto a paper-lined or lightly greased pan, using a tablespoon for about a 2-inch cookie (these are factors you can control). Space pieces of dough about 1 inch apart to allow for spreading during baking. Bake at 385 degrees. The yield—the outcome—is 4 dozen cookies.

In recipes, it's easy to define the independent, dependent, and control variables and the desired outcome. In social work, it's also important to be able to look at any research question and be able to break it down into its different factors.

Evaluating Practice

The Curriculum Policy Statement also mentions the goal of evaluating practice. But what does that mean? To put it in systems terminology, our output (the actual end product) should equal our desired outcome (the anticipated end product). Once we know what we want to achieve from the interaction, it is possible to ascertain whether we achieved it. However, many times we may not really know what we want as a result, so it is hard to determine whether we achieved a desired outcome.

Let me use pizza to demonstrate this concept. There are so many different types of pizza. Just listen to the commercials—thin crust, thick crust, stuffed crust, and so on, let alone the various toppings. So, if someone said to you, "Let's go out for pizza!" would you know what you will end up eating? Evaluating practice is very much like going out for pizza; it is important to know what you want before you go out for it. Below is a basic recipe for pizza dough and another for sauce. Feel free to experiment with the toppings and the types of crust that you would like, but remember, you need some idea of what you want your pizza to taste like before you start—you need to know what you want before you can evaluate the outcome.

Pizza Dough

1 tsp salt	4–6 cups flour
1 tbsp sugar	1 tbsp shortening (optional)
1 package dry yeast	Garlic and basil to taste to
1½ cups water	vary the crust

Mix all the ingredients together. When using dry yeast follow the directions on the package regarding water temperature and mixing with sugar before adding flour. Usually the water should be about 110 degrees (or warm to your touch). If the water is too hot it will kill the yeast or if too cold the yeast will not activate properly. Mix for about 10 minutes. Let the dough rest for about 20 to 30 minutes, and then cut it into pieces for your pizzas. This recipe makes two 16-inch pies. Round the pieces of dough. Flatten them by hand and then roll out the dough to about $\frac{1}{8}$-inch thick. The dough should be slightly thicker at the edges than the center as this will create a rim that will contain the topping during baking.

Pizza Sauce

1 can of tomato puree	$\frac{1}{4}$ tsp basil
1 tsp salt	$\frac{1}{4}$ tsp oregano
$\frac{1}{2}$ tsp sugar	$\frac{1}{4}$ tsp garlic
$\frac{1}{8}$ tsp pepper	

Mix all the ingredients and bring them to a slow simmer. Allow the sauce to cook slowly for about 15 minutes. The sauce should be of gravy consistency and cooled before it's added to the dough (hot or warm sauce will make the dough soggy). Use about 6 to 7 ounces of sauce per 16-inch pizza.

Top the pizza with ground or shredded mozzarella cheese. Use about 8 ounces per 16-inch pizza. Then top with whatever vegetables or other toppings you desire.

Bake in a hot oven. If you are making thin crust (Neapolitan), it should be baked at 500 degrees for about 10 minutes. A thick crust (Sicilian) is baked in a deep pan. Bake it at 450 degrees for about 15 minutes. You can check to see if the pizza is done by carefully lifting the dough and checking, making sure not to have the topping run over the edge.

When conducting research, we begin with a basic thought or hypothesis. We then figure out how to test our hypothesis, to see if its conclusions are valid. If what we expect does happen, the hypothesis is correct and tested. (Often, we don't test hypotheses but test the converse of the hypothesis, or the null hypothesis. If we disprove the null hypothesis, we assume that the hypothesis is correct, or what we expected.) For example, consider cheesecake.

Before we take that first bite, we have an idea of what the cheese-cake will taste like. If it tastes the way we thought or better, then we have "proved our hypothesis" and declare it a good cheesecake. On the other hand, if it does not taste like we think it should, we may say it's not a good cheesecake or even that it's a bad (wrong) cheesecake. That is, evaluation is based on preconceived outcomes before the experiment is begun.

So, what is your preconception of cheesecake? How does that preconception affect your evaluation of the cheesecake in the following recipe?

Cheesecake Crust

1 cup of graham crackers (approx. 11 cracker sheets)

½ cup of margarine, melted

¼ cup of granulated sugar

Crush, or grind, the graham crackers and then mix with the sugar. Stir together with the melted margarine. Press into a 10-inch spring form pan.

Sour Cream Cheesecake

1½ lb cream cheese

5 oz sour cream

1 cup of sugar

3 tbsp flour

pinch of salt

1 tsp vanilla or other flavoring

½ cup eggs (3 eggs)

Mix ingredients together. Pour into the graham cracker crust. Bake for 35 minutes at 350 degrees.

Critical Thinking Prompts

- Identify a social problem or question that you would like to have answered.

- Identify the component parts of that problem, the independent, dependent, and control variables relating to the problem.

- What measures could you use to determine whether you were able to successfully answer the problem/question?

CHAPTER 3

Human Behavior in the Social Environment

WHAT'S IN THIS CHAPTER:

- Definition of human behavior in the social environment
- Discussion of human interactions
- Description of bio-psycho-social factors that affect people
- Description of person in environment
- Discussion about the relationship between theory and practice

F urr (1997) uses a fish metaphor to help students understand human behavior in the social environment. He asks students how they would study a particular species of fish. If they catch the fish and try to study it on the deck of the boat, then they are overlooking the fish's environment—the ocean—and its interactions with the other creatures in its environment. Studying people is like studying the fish in the ocean. To understand people, they should be studied in their environment. That is why human behavior in the social environment (HBSE) is an important curricular content area within social work. "The overall purpose of teaching human development in social work is to introduce students to the complex interplay of the biological, psychological, social, and spiritual factors that together find expression in the marvels of humanity" (Reid, Rodwell, & Bricout, 1997, p. 9).

This purpose has been translated by the Council on Social Work Education as a standard that governs all accredited social work programs. This standard states that all "programs must provide content about theories and knowledge of human bio-psycho-social development, including theories and knowledge about the range of social systems in which individuals live (families, groups, organizations, institutions, and communities). The human behavior and the social environment curriculum must provide an understanding of the interactions between and among human biological, social, psychological, and cultural systems as they affect and are affected by human behavior" (Council on Social Work Education, 1994, pp. 102, 140).

There are a lot of different concepts in the CSWE statement. Probably most evident is providing "content about theories and knowledge of human bio-psycho-social development" and social systems. Actually, there are many such theories, far too many to identify all of them in this book. However, I will identify some of them and present food analogies to explain them.

The CSWE statement implies that there is a theory or rationale about everything that social workers do. Some theories are based on biological factors that explain how individuals behave. Other theories involve psychological factors that contribute to the person's behavior. And still others relate to the culture or sources outside the individual that also contribute to behavior. Since humans are recognized as social beings, they interact with others in a social environment. In social work, that is called the person-in-environment fit. In order to understand the person-in-environment fit, it is important to understand some of the theories that explain that fit. This section will present some of those theories with recipes that may help you understand the discussion.

The Social Environment

As discussed in Chapter 1, on the concept of the ecological systems perspective, all interactions and relationships among people happen within the context of a larger social environment. The social environment is defined as "all the influences, conditions, and natural surroundings that affect the growth and development of living things" (Barker, 1995, p. 121). Because human beings are social beings, it is impossible to understand people outside the social environment. Therefore, it is important to understand the context within which we are studying people.

Some authors refer to individuals as *microsystems*. When referring to the social environment, these authors use the terms *mezzo* and *macrosystems*. These are simply size delineations. *Mezzo* refers to the small group environments in which people interact, the groups that have some level of direct interaction with the individual, such as family, school, church/synagogue, or social group. *Macrosystems* refer to larger environmental systems that do not directly interact with the individual but that will have an indirect effect on the behavior of the person (Friedman, 1997). Macrosystems are often those where policies are made that indirectly affect people. As mentioned in Chapter 1, the altitude of a location affects the way things bake; the altitude would be considered a macrosystem. Similarly, communities, government, and even religious movements—all macrosystems—establish policies that indirectly influence the way we interact with others.

Thus, we cannot study an individual without looking at the individual's social environment of family, friends, and policies that are influencing the individual's interactions. Because people are social beings, we may find that we are furthering our understanding not of the individual but of the way that the individual interacts with others. In order to do so, it is important to understand the context or the social environment of the person.

Looking at Human Interactions

Social work involves the interactions of people. Brill (1995, p. 31) states: "The individual exists in interrelationships with other people and with all other life forms. This relationship may be defined as one of mutual rights and responsibilities." That is, people are social beings and interact with one another in the course of their lives. Human development is dependent upon the nature of the interaction between one person and another. How are these interactions perceived?

I like to think of human interactions as salad dressing. The two main ingredients in salad dressing are oil and vinegar. Each by itself is a good, solid product that can stand on its own. However, the interaction of the two creates a different product that we use to flavor salads—salad dressing. The interesting thing about salad dressing is that since the two main ingredients, oil and vinegar, do not naturally mix, we need to work the salad dressing, usually by shaking, before using it. If the dressing is left unattended, the two main ingredients separate.

Relationships are like salad dressing. At the simplest level they involve two people. It takes work for these two individuals to develop a relationship. And some sort of interaction is necessary in order for the relationship to be successful. If the relationship is left unattended, then the individuals separate. The interactions between people create a new product, a relationship.

The following recipe represents a relationship between ingredients. It is necessary to work this relationship by mixing (shaking) before using it in order to maintain the integrity of the relationship as an end product.

Balsamic Vinaigrette Salad Dressing

¼ cup balsamic vinegar   1 to 2 garlic cloves (crushed)

⅓ cup extra virgin olive oil   salt and pepper to taste

1 tsp basil

Place all ingredients in a shaker bottle. Shake and serve over a salad.

Of course, salad dressing is only effective if it is used with something, usually a salad. The salad might be called the social environment for the dressing. The recipe above should be used within a lettuce environment where an oil and vinaigrette dressing would be appropriate. In other environments, such as a fruit salad, you would not want to use an oil and vinegar dressing.

Relationships are very much the same in that they are dependent on the environment. Two people may interact well, with some work, within one environment but not in another. Think about the various places where you meet people and how you interact with them, depending on the environment. Do you act the same way with everyone, or do your actions depend on the situation? Thus, relationships, like salad dressing, need both work on the interaction between the people or ingredients and the right environment.

Biological Theories

The individual is a very complex being, consisting of cells and organs. In order for the body to function properly, there is a need for all of these cells and organs to interact appropriately. Brill (1995, p. 31) states, "Each person and all living things are characterized by a need to grow and develop toward realization of a unique potential." As part of this growth process, each person, whether consciously or not, changes. Germain (1991) refers to this as adaptation and relates it to a cause-and-effect process that people experience: "Adaptation may be directed to changing oneself in order to meet environmental opportunities or demands, or it may be directed to changing the environment so that physical and social settings will be more responsive to human needs, rights, goals, and capacities" (p. 17).

There is a normal body chemistry that contributes to our health and our behavior. We can control some of our body chemistry through nutritional behaviors in watching what we eat and the vitamins we take. For example, some factors, like cholesterol, we can control to some extent by controlling our diet. Some, like smoking, we can also control. But others—such as blood type, height, skin color—are genetic "givens"; we must learn to live with them. One area where we can exercise control is in the substances we choose to use or not use to alter our normal state of consciousness (Doweiko, 1996). Do people abuse substances because of some genetic factor (the nature argument) or because of something in their environment (peer pressure, perhaps—the nurture argument). So far, the evidence does not point to one factor more than the other. That is why it is important to have a grounding in both, to understand that there may be times when behavior emerges from a biological condition (perhaps a chemical imbalance) and other times when it may have environmental causes.

Recent studies have determined that our bodies generate chemicals called endorphins that moderate emotions and behaviors in people (Doweiko, 1996). Endorphins are generated naturally when someone is in a positive relationship or in love. Chocolate is said to have some of the same properties that endorphins do. Have you ever felt a little low and eaten a candy bar and felt better? Some of that mood elevation was caused by the endorphin-like effect of the chocolate in your body. (Of course, some people need other chemicals, perhaps a prescribed antidepressant, to regulate their moods. And certain conditions may require a combination of treatment modalities.)

But, for most of us, a chocolate cake will elevate our mood and provide a reminder of how important it is to consider biological factors when working with people. And because a cake is something that is usually shared, we can use the cake to enhance our social environment.

Chocolate Cake

⅔ cup shortening	1¼ cups cocoa powder
1½ cups granulated sugar	1¼ cups water
1½ tbsp baking powder	3 eggs
2 tsp baking soda	3 tsp vanilla
2 cups flour	1 tsp salt

In an electric mixer, mix all ingredients together at low speed for 2 minutes and then at medium speed for 5 minutes. Pour into two 9-inch cake pans. Bake in a moderate oven (350 degrees) for 30 to 35 minutes. Let the cake cool for 10 minutes and then remove it from the pan.

A plain chocolate cake is just that, plain. It needs icing to make it a cake. I find that it is easiest to ice a cake when the cake is frozen. So once you remove the cake from the pan, put it on a cookie sheet and let it freeze for at least 8 hours. There are many types of icings you can use; the one below is for a basic buttercream icing that can be used when decorating any cake.

Basic Buttercream Icing

1 lb confectioners' sugar	1 tsp vanilla or almond
1 cup solid vegetable	extract
shortening	2 tbsp clear corn syrup
2 tbsp water	

Sift the confectioners' sugar into a large mixing bowl. Add the remaining ingredients and blend until all the ingredients are thoroughly mixed. Mix an additional minute. If using an electric mixer, mix at medium speed making sure not to overbeat. Use the icing at room temperature.

Since you have two 9-inch cakes, you can layer them to create one larger cake. To do so, you need to make sure the tops of the cake layers are flat. (The bottoms are already flat from the cake pans.) With a large knife (such as a bread knife), slice the bulge off the top of each cake layer. Spread icing on the top of one layer. Flip the other layer upside down on top of the first layer so that the two tops are touching with icing to hold them together. Then, using either a regular dinner knife or a cake knife, spread the remaining icing over the cake, covering the sides and what is now the top. The icing seals the moisture into the cake. The cake can then be eaten anytime within 24 hours.

Maslow's Motivation Theory

Maslow (1970) believed that individuals must have their basic survival/physiological needs met before they can move on to take care of safety and security needs and finally achieve self-esteem and self-actualization.

Because people are interactional, relationships exist between people. A relationship can be one in which one person is dependent on another, such as an infant depending on his or her mother for fulfilling basic survival needs. Or the individuals in a relationship can be interdependent, which allows each person to maintain his or her unique identity yet work in conjunction with others as part of the relationship (Covey, 1989).

In essence, Maslow stated that an individual is motivated toward certain behaviors as a result of the necessity for fulfilling needs in a certain order. Only after the lower-order needs have been met can a person then move on to the next, higher-order need.

Consider the current social problem of homelessness. A homeless person's most basic needs are for food and for shelter. Only when those needs are met—by shelters for the homeless or by other means—can the homeless person move on to taking care of the higher-level need for safety and security. Many homeless people will not go to the shelters because they feel the shelters are not safe (Friedman, 1993). This need for safety—along with the basic physiological needs—must be fulfilled, and some level of comfort reached, before individuals begin to invite others into interdependent relationships. Food is a very social item that lends itself to interactions with others. In moving up Maslow's hierarchy of needs, the homeless individual will first prepare simple foods representing basic-level needs. As the individual becomes more competent and comfortable, he or she will begin to experiment and prepare more difficult dishes representing a move toward self-esteem. What is self-actualization, the highest level of need?

I like to think of self-actualization as the garnish or the icing on the cake. The cake by itself is fine, but the icing makes it complete—the cake reaches its fullest potential with icing. Garnishes add to the presentation of food and make the plate look "finished," complete. Thus, self-actualization is the difference between having a full life and feeling that one is merely subsisting on a day-to-day basis. The recipe below demonstrates interdependence among ingredients. Each fruit by itself is a whole product. When the different fruits interact, they form a salad, and the topping raises the salad to a finished, self-actualized, state.

Holyland Fruit Salad

Use ½ cup of each of the following fruits from the Middle East (vary this according to your tastes):

pears	raisins
peaches	apples
pineapple	4 oz whipping cream
guavas	or 2 egg whites
oranges	½ cup curaçao
cherries	

Pour curaçao over the cherries and raisins and let them soak.
Dice the fruit and mix the diced fruit with the soaked cherries and raisins. Chill and serve in champagne glasses. Beat
whipping cream or egg whites, until stiff peaks are formed.
(Canned whipping cream can also be used.) Top the fruit
with the whipped cream or egg whites. Garnish with a
strawberry or cherry. When fresh fruit is not available, use
canned fruit. If some fresh fruit is available, mix it with the
canned.

The Range of Social Systems

The CSWE standard states that programs should discuss theories about a range of social systems. It specifically identifies
families, groups, organizations, institutions, and communities.
There are developmental theories that discuss individuals as
if they live in isolation. However, all individuals interact with
others, and their behavior is dependent on the values of
the groups within which they function (their ecological environment). These groups, or systems, are usually classified
as micro (individual), mezzo (family/groups), and/or macro
(community).

Well, food can be classified the same way. For example, when
you are making a bread recipe you can take a strip of dough and
roll it out. By itself, it can be one bread stick. But if you take, for
example, four of the bread sticks and braid them together, you
can create a whole loaf or a *challah* (a braided bread). The whole
loaf becomes more than the sum of its ingredients, or parts, just
as a group is different from the individual members who com-
pose it (Chess & Norlin, 1991). So, we take individual ingredients and create a new whole—the challah or group. But the
challah is only part of a larger meal. We can consider the entire
meal, where the challah is now another part, as a community, the
social setting in which individuals (people as well as bread)
function.

Challah

I tsp salt

⅓ cup sugar

2 tbsp shortening

1–2 packages dry yeast

I cup water

3 eggs

4–6 cups flour

Follow the directions on the dry yeast package regarding water temperature and mixing with sugar before adding flour. Then mix all the ingredients together for about 10 minutes. Let the dough rise for 1 to 2 hours in a warm place. Divide in two, and take a pastry brush and paint each with egg wash and let both halves rise again for about 1 to 2 hours. Wash the halves with egg wash a second time before baking. Bake in a moderate oven, 350 degrees, for about 20 minutes.

Directions for Braiding Challah (Four Braids)

Make four strands, seal at the top. Think of the strands as A, B, C, D. (See figure below.) Create a space between B and C. Take A in your left hand and D in your right. Bring D across B and C. Bring A down the middle between B and C, crossing D and B. Take B and cross A and C. Bring D into the middle between A and C, crossing A. Take C and cross A and D, bring B into the middle between A and D. Take A across B and D, bring C into the middle between B and D. Continue until the strands are completed.

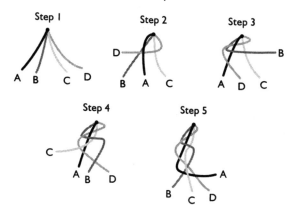

Integrating Theory and Practice

To this point a couple of theories have been introduced that relate to social work practice. Remember, the previous chapter mentioned that social work practice is a scientific process, a process that derives from theory. The ecological systems perspective is a way of organizing different pieces of information, but it still does not explain what you are seeing. Therefore, it is important to know a variety of theories that you can use to give some meaning to your observations as you look at the person in the environment. Some theories may apply to the individual, whereas others may apply to the environment within which the individual exists. All theories provide some rationale to explain why a client system acts in the way that it does.

One of the best aspects of social work is that there is an organizing perspective, the ecological systems perspective, and we borrow theories from other disciplines to help explain what is happening within the system. We can borrow theories from psychology, sociology, economics, anthropology, political science, biology, chemistry, religion, or any other field. This truly helps provide a liberal arts perspective to social work education. If you are observing something that does not seem to make sense, then it is time to explore the literature for theories that can help explain your observations. The observed behavior may actually be understood by the interaction of multiple theories. Inquire and use a scientific process in applying theory to practice.

Critical Thinking Prompts

■ Provide your own metaphor for defining human behavior in the social environment.

■ How would you describe "person in the environment"?

■ Identify some foods that have an effect on your behavior. List them and their effects.

- Maslow says that people need to meet lower-order needs before moving to higher-order needs. He calls his theory a motivational theory as one is only motivated to move to a higher-order need once the lower-order need has been satisfied. Do you agree? Have you found motivations even when your basic needs are not fully satisfied? What were your motivating factors?

- Within social work you will learn a variety of theories that relate to human behavior. Identify two other theories and discuss their relevance to social work practice.

CHAPTER 4

Social Work Practice

WHAT'S IN THIS CHAPTER:

- Discussion of social work practice
- Description of the concept of conscious use of self
- Description of basic skills needed in practice
- Review of the problem-solving process

he essence of social work is the practice of addressing the welfare of people within society, thus the term *social* (society) *welfare*. "By the time people began to live in groups and leave some record of their existence, there was evidence of concern for the common welfare (which meant concern for all people) and of working together to insure it, even if this cooperation involved nothing more than allocation of tasks on the basis of differential abilities" (Brill, 1995, p. 2). Approximately 100 years ago, the first professional social work training program was developed. The professionals so trained are called social workers. "Social workers strive to create order and enhance opportunities for people in an increasingly complex world" (Miley, O'Melia, & DuBois, 1998, p. 1). How social workers learn the practice of social work is dictated by the Council on Social Work Education (1994) in its Curriculum Policy Statement (CPS), which states:

> Social work practice must include knowledge, values, and skills to enhance the well-being of people and to help ameliorate the environmental conditions that affect people adversely. Practice content must include the following skills: defining issues; collecting and assessing data; planning and contracting; identifying alternative interventions; selecting and implementing appropriate courses of action; using appropriate research to monitor and evaluate outcomes; applying appropriate research-based knowledge and technological advances; and termination. (pp. 102, 141)

From a pedagogical perspective, practice is one of the most difficult areas of the curriculum to conceptualize (Hoffman & Sallee, 1994). There is the complexity of the range of issues that professionals are called upon to address when working with people. In addition, there are a number of ways to address an issue, from working individually with a person to striving to make large-scale institutional changes that will affect everyone in society. This chapter will briefly address some of the basic concepts relating to practice and explain them through the use of metaphors.

Social work practice is the teaching of skills in order to help people. Within social work, the term *skill* refers to "being proficient in communication, assessing problems and client workability, matching *needs* and *resources*, developing resources, and changing social structures" (Barker, 1995, p. 349; italics in original). In performing these skills the social worker should follow a logical scientific process. "To practice social work effectively, specific knowledge and mastery of a variety of intervention approaches are needed. The social worker not only must be able to work directly with a client or clients, but also should be prepared to understand and work to change the environment of these clients" (Morales & Sheafor, 1998, p. 43).

So let's look at some of the logical processes and intervention strategies of social work. As in baking and cooking, it is one thing to place everything in a bowl, mix them up, and then cook or bake the mixture. As you know, you need a rationale for the ingredients used, how they are mixed, and the temperature and length of time they are cooked. The recipe is the scientific rationale, just as the training one receives as a social worker will provide the skills and knowledge to be able to assess a situation and to make appropriate interventions at the appropriate times to achieve a desired result. Most of the time, the training is a logical process based on theory. However, social work requires skill in practice in order to accomplish desired results. These practice skills are processes that are practiced until the technique becomes second nature in your actions as a professional.

Before discussing some specific skills, I'd like to present a basic overview of the learning process. When a field is unfamiliar or new to people, they begin at a point of unconscious incompetence. That is, they do not know that they do not know. Once they realize that they do not know, they move to a level of conscious incompetence. Now they are aware that there is information they do not know and that in order to perform these new tasks they need to develop a level of skill to achieve them. People now work at becoming competent and strive to achieve a level of conscious competence. After they repeat the techniques a number of times, they move to a level of unconscious competence; that is, the action becomes second nature, almost automatic, in that they can now perform the task without having to consciously think about what they are doing.

As professionals, it is important to always be aware of our actions and the effects they have. Therefore, even performing as a social worker may become second nature, it is always possible to pull into consciousness the rationale for why we perform a process to achieve a desired result. This is called the *conscious use of self.*

Conscious Use of Self

One of the differences between cooking and baking and social work is the nature of the skills used. Within cooking and baking, there are tools and physical skills that a person needs to acquire in order to apply the recipe and achieve a desired result. Within social work the skills are primarily cognitive and the vehicle for the intervention is the professional. Cournoyer (1996) defines social work skills as "a set of discrete cognitive and behavioral actions that (1) derive from social work knowledge and from social work values, ethics, and obligations, (2) are consistent with the essential facilitative qualities, and (3) comport with a social work purpose within the context of a phase of practice" (p. 4). To effectuate a beneficial intervention, professionals have to understand themselves, their strengths and weaknesses, and always pay attention to the quality of the interaction with the client system in order to achieve a desired outcome. In addition, professionals need to be conscious of whatever biases may arise as a result of the interaction with the client system.

Defining Issues

The first skill identified by the CPS is defining issues. In essence what this means is that the social worker has to be able to understand the real problem. This involves breaking the problem into manageable parts.

To put this another way, when a client system has a problem it is usually because the system is overwhelmed with aspects in life.

Remember the old saying that a person often cannot see the forest for the trees? Well, often this is part of the problem. In effect, the client system cannot see the forest for the trees or is overwhelmed by all the trees.

Social workers will help the client system understand the problem by helping to define the issues. This is a skill where questions are asked that break the problem into pieces, a process called *partializing*. Once all the pieces have been identified it is possible to ask questions that will help to identify what the client system wants to have resolved. Thus, defining the problem is the first overriding skill social workers need to develop. (Of course, social workers also need to develop interviewing skills to be able to accomplish the defining the problem stage of the intervention. We will look at the skills that are part of this process in the next section, "Collecting and Assessing Data.")

When we cook or bake, it is also important to define the "issues." This is done by knowing the ingredients that make up the final product and the order in which they are used in the recipe. Timing is another important factor. If we do all the right steps but our timing is off, then things will not be done when we want them to be. This is certainly an issue when preparing a full meal. For example, if we are preparing a rice and stir-fry dinner, we should not start the stir-fry part before the rice. Rice takes about a half hour to cook whereas the stir-fry takes minutes. So, timing is very important when cooking. In both cooking and in social work, there is a preliminary step before beginning. This is the necessity to assess the situation and define the problem. Once the problem has been defined then it is possible to develop an appropriate intervention.

To demonstrate the concept of defining issues, let me introduce a metaphor—a Chinese dinner. You want to cook and serve Chinese food. You want everything to be done at the same time and not have your guests wait while you prepare part of the meal. So, you identify the problem, in this case the cooking times of the various parts of the meal, and then work backward to have everything prepared together. You know that the rice takes about a half hour. Therefore, you begin with the rice.

Rice

1 cup of long- or short-grain white rice (brown rice may also be used but then add 10 minutes to the cooking time)

2 cups cold water

1 tbsp powdered chicken consommé or 1 cube chicken bouillon

Put the rice, water, and chicken soup flavor in a sauce pan (about 1½ quart size for this amount of rice). Bring the water to a boil and stir occasionally. Once the water boils, turn the heat down to warm or low and cover the pot. Set a timer for 20 minutes and let the rice continue cooking in the covered pot. After 20 minutes, turn off the burner and let the pot sit for another 5 minutes. Do not remove the cover. Once the 25 minutes is over, take the cover off. The water should all be absorbed and the rice should be tender. Yield: 3 cups.

Stir-Fry Vegetables

2 tbsp oil

2 garlic cloves minced

1 tsp dried ginger (or fresh, chopped ginger)

1 medium onion, chopped

2 carrots

1 lb frozen broccoli and cauliflower mixture (or other frozen vegetables)

½ clear chicken broth or consommé

½ cup soy sauce

2 tbsp cornstarch

While the rice is cooking, heat your wok with the oil (a regular frying pan can be used if you don't have a wok). When the oil is hot (splatters when you put a drop of water in it), add the garlic and ginger. Brown the garlic and ginger and then add the chopped onions. Let the onions brown and then add the rest of the vegetable ingredients. Stir until tender. Add the chicken broth and let everything cook for about 2 minutes. While the vegetables are cooking with the chicken broth, mix the soy sauce and cornstarch together to create a paste. Add this paste to the vegetable mixture in the wok and stir. This will thicken the mixture. Serve over the steamed rice.

These recipes demonstrate that by understanding a specific process or problem, it is possible to partialize the situation and arrive at a technique to find solutions to the parts to create a solution for the meal (or problem) itself.

Collecting and Assessing Data

The word *data* may sound scary, but it just means collecting information about a situation. Every type of information gathering is a collection of data. Yet there is a skill in collecting data. We cannot just sit down and expect the data to flow. As social workers, we need to apply communication skills—active listening and empathy in particular—so that we can gather information about a client in order to be able to determine (assess) what is affecting the client both as an individual and as a member of a larger group.

Active listening skills are an important component of communication and an integral part of the skills needed in the helping process. "Active listening combines the talking and listening skills in such a way that clients feel understood and encouraged toward further self-expression" (Cournoyer, 1996, p. 93). Through active listening, the social worker is able to gain an understanding of what the client is expressing as his or her problem. This is the data that the worker needs in order to begin the steps of problem solving.

Empathy is another skill that is needed to assist in the data collection process. Empathy is a difficult concept to understand and one that many professionals need to constantly develop throughout their careers and in each client interaction. Sheafor, Horejsi, and Horejsi (1997) describe empathy by stating, "one must get inside that person's thoughts, beliefs, and life experiences. But before that is possible, one must first set aside his or her own values, attitudes, and judgments" (p. 38). The skill of being able to set aside one's own values, attitudes, and judgments in order to be able to understand the other person in an unbiased manner is easier said than done, but it is a necessary skill to being able to gain a true understanding of the data (information) being communicated by the client system. Helping students gain an appreciation of empathy is one of the reasons that methods courses are difficult to teach, for it is easy to teach theory, but to begin to apply that theory until it becomes part of one's skills takes a lot of practice. It is part of the growth process that all social workers experience and why social workers continue to learn even when they have been practicing for years.

Although it may not seem like it, there is a correlation between food preparation and data collection. We only need to realize that food serves two important purposes. First, it is a source of sustenance, and, second, it is part of socializing. Food can be eaten alone. However, it is much more fun to eat with other people. And, food is often a reason for getting together or socializing. But whether one prepares food for guests or chooses to go out with a group to eat, it is important to take into consideration the special dietary needs of the other people in the group. Sometimes these dietary needs are religiously based, or health motivated, or simply personal preferences. By *attending* to special dietary needs we use our sense of empathy. For example, some people are allergic to any type of nut. Most banana breads or cakes include walnuts. If any of your guests have this food allergy, it is important to take it into consideration and prepare banana cake or bread without nuts. In addition, most banana cake or bread recipes include sour cream or some type of dairy product. This would not be appropriate for those individuals who are lactose intolerant or who keep kosher and do not want to mix meat and milk at a meal. Therefore, I have adapted a killer banana cake recipe that has been in my family for years to accommodate these special needs. This act of attending to special needs is part of the skill of empathy.

Banana Cake

½ cup shortening	I tsp vanilla
I cup sugar	I ½ cups flour
2 eggs	I tsp baking soda
2 overripe bananas	

Preheat the oven to 350 degrees. Cream sugar and shortening together. Add eggs, vanilla, and bananas and mix. Then mix in the flour and baking soda. Pour into a greased and floured tube pan (9-cup) and bake for 50 minutes. If making muffins, the baking time will be 30 minutes. Yield: 12 muffins.

Planning and Contracting

Planning and contracting are important concepts within social work, as in other aspects of life. Planning relates to the ability to anticipate events and activities. It is to be proactive rather than re-active. Within social work, this relates to using the information on hand to be able to perceive potential situations before they happen and to develop some alternative solutions if problems do arise. This is the prevention model of social work practice.

Prevention is an important concept within social work practice. "*Prevention* involves the timely provision of services to vulnerable persons, promoting social functioning before problems develop, and includes programs and activities such as family planning, well-baby clinics, parent education, premarital and preretirement counseling, and marital enrichment programs" (Hepworth, Rooney, & Larsen, 1997, p. 5; italics added). That is, planning involves making provisions to prevent anticipated problems. As a social worker, it is our responsibility not only to help clients problem solve but also to provide assistance so that clients develop skills that address future problems before they occur, or can anticipate problems and develop strategies to address them. I often say, "It is our job to put ourselves out of a job." For a client system to become self-reliant and not dependent, the client must learn to plan for the unexpected.

This model also applies to meal preparation. We have to anticipate (plan) what we will be making before starting to prepare the meal. We must make sure that the proper ingredients are available and that there is proper time to prepare the meal. Without planning, there may be problems when it becomes time to prepare or serve the meal.

Contracting is also an important aspect of social work practice. "Contracting follows integrally from the assessment process. It yields clearly identified problems, specific goals for work, a change program for pursuing the goals, and, often, one or more discrete action steps" (Cournoyer, 1996, p. 246). Contracting involves developing an agreement between you, the worker, and the client system, whether the client is an individual, family, group, or community. The nature of the agreement establishes parameters so that everyone understands what she or he is to do and has an understanding of what will be achieved as a result of the interactions. When these roles are not understood, problems may arise because one person's expectations were different from the other. Contracting is the formal method used to agree on the anticipated outcomes of interactions among different people.

For example, it is difficult to work with an entire family when only part of the family attends sessions. Therefore, it is necessary to contract with the family so that all family members attend. I worked for one agency where the entire family was required to attend the initial session or they would not be served. That is one way social workers use contracts. Another would be to contract the number of times that you plan to meet with the client system. For instance, in developing a minimum-contact, multidimensional, smoking-cessation program, the participants knew that they would have to come for only five sessions. Following the five sessions, they had the opportunity to extend the duration of the group, but that entailed a modification to the contract. Contracts are agreements between worker and client system that are agreed upon by both parties.

Food preparation involves both planning and contracting. That is, it's important not only to plan your preparation but also to contract with others about what you are going to make. Since food is a source of socializing, it is important that everyone is clear about the type of food that is expected.

Cheesecake is a dessert that involves contracting. When I think of cheesecake, I think of many varieties. Cheesecake has become something of a very personal choice, ranging from heavy to light texture from baked to not baked. Thus, when someone asks for cheesecake, I find it's important to ask what type of cheesecake the person would like, or that we contract about the cheesecake. Below is one of my favorite specialty cheesecake recipes. It is a light-textured, baked cheesecake. Try contracting with your friends about which kind of cheesecake (this one or the recipe in Chapter 2) you should make.

Amaretto Cheesecake

1 lb cream cheese	¾ cup cream
5 eggs, separated	¼ cup Amaretto
2 tbsp flour	(other flavors can be
1 cup sugar	substituted)

Beat egg whites until stiff. Mix the rest of the ingredients until the mixture is smooth. Fold in egg whites. Place in graham cracker crust (see recipe in Chapter 2). Bake at 325 degrees for 1 hour. Serves 8 to 12.

Using the Problem-Solving Process

If we look at the role of all social workers as that of being a change agent (that is, as involved with changing something that currently exists within the client system), then it is important to understand the client's strengths, what resources within the client and the environment can be drawn upon in order to develop solutions that will resolve present and future problems. In addition, if we truly believe that all systems are unique then there is not a single solution for all problems. As a social worker, it is our job to be able to identify those unique aspects within the client system and to assist the client system to explore alternatives that will lead to some resolution of the problem. Finding solutions is called the problem-solving process.

The problem-solving process is the framework for finding a strategy to implement the change process (Hepworth, Rooney, & Larsen, 1997). By linking the process to the contract, the client learns strategies to address future problems.

First, it is important to realize that client systems will seek help when there is a problem. It is also important, as a social worker, to help the client system identify the problem that brought them in for help. Once the problem has been identified, then you, as the worker, contract with the client system, specifying the number of sessions and who needs to be involved as part of the interventions to obtain a solution to the problem. The contracting becomes part of the problem-solving process. For example, I worked with a couple in marital counseling who were struggling with problems of intimacy and premature ejaculation by the husband. To help them begin to see how their relationship had developed, I asked them to explain what typically transpired at the dinner table. When they both related that dinner was usually served and eaten quickly so each could go on to other endeavors, I contracted with them to go to the slowest-service restaurant in town and experience a leisurely meal. The following week they returned and told me that the dinner had lasted three hours. They also said that they had the best sexual experience in years following that dinner. Here the contract was the homework assignment that the client system performed, and it led to a solution to the problem.

There are eight steps to the problem-solving process. These include:

Identifying the problem

Selecting goals

Generating alternatives
Weighing consequences
Deciding
Planning
Implementing
Evaluating

Identifying Alternative Interventions

It is always important to identify alternative solutions to the problem and then to weigh the consequences, for there are a variety of different ways to resolve a problem. As social workers we need to clarify which alternative method seems to relate most closely to the strengths and skills of the client.

Alternative interventions are important concepts within food preparation as well. With people becoming more conscious of health issues, there has been a move to reducing or removing fats and cholesterol from the food we eat. Today we have alternatives for many common foods, though there is still the question of whether taste has been sacrificed for health. Presently, the bagel has surpassed the doughnut as a breakfast food. Even Dunkin Donuts has begun carrying a line of bagels because of their popularity and their health benefits over doughnuts. But there is some debate about the health effects of different kinds of bagels. There are egg bagels, which tend to be a little softer because of the fat in the egg yolks, and there are water bagels. Thus, if a bagel is part of your breakfast, then you have alternatives. Below are recipes for both water and egg bagels. As you will note, the recipes are very similar with the difference being that the eggs are replaced by water in the water bagel. The water causes a slightly different consistency and color. Although the recipes are different, the method of preparation is the same.

Bagels

Water Bagels	*Egg Bagels*
1 tsp salt	1 tsp salt
⅓ cup sugar	⅓ cup sugar
¼ cup oil	¼ cup oil
1¾ cups warm water	½ cup eggs (about 3 eggs)
1½ packages dry yeast or 1½ oz cake yeast	1¼ cups warm water
4 cups flour	1½ package dry yeast or 1½ oz cake yeast
	4 cups flour

Place the salt, sugar, oil, water, and yeast in a bowl. Add about half the flour and mix thoroughly. This will begin the process of activating the yeast. Continue mixing, and add the rest of the flour. The dough should be smooth and elastic and a little sticky but not too sticky. Let the dough rest about a half hour. Then cut the dough into pieces—a normal bagel is about 2 ounces, so you can cut the dough into 2-ounce pieces. (For minibagels, cut into smaller pieces; for larger bagels, cut into larger pieces.) Roll each piece into a cylinder and then connect the two ends together to form a circle. Place each circle on a cookie sheet and let them rest about a half hour. In the meantime bring a pot of water to a boil. When the water is at a rolling boil, drop each bagel into the boiling water. The bagel will first sink to the bottom of the pot but will then rise to the surface. When the bagel has risen to the surface, remove it from the water and place it on a cookie sheet lined with parchment paper. Bake the bagels in a hot oven (about 425 degrees) for about 12 to 15 minutes or until the tops and bottoms are brown.

Selecting and Implementing Appropriate Courses of Action

Once the social worker has identified alternative solutions, it is important to work with the client system in helping the client system develop an appropriate action step. This may be difficult at times because our value system may be in conflict with the action that the client system chooses. However, a social work value is that of client self-determination, which loosely means that it is up to the client system to make the choice without coercion by the social worker. The social worker can present alternatives, but the final decision is up to the client system. Many refer to this as the worker empowering the client.

A goal of helping professionals is to assist clients to gain power over their lives or empower them to gain control. "Use of the term *empowerment* to capture this commitment to working collaboratively with people to attain their goals by increasing their personal and political power to influence their life situations has gained prominence in recent years" (Sheafor, Horejsi, & Horejsi, 1997, p. 80). Of course, choosing a course of action is different from carrying out the action steps themselves. But, at any rate, it is important that the decision is the client system's choice and not based on what the social worker feels is best for the client system. The social worker acts as a facilitator in the decision process (Carkhuff & Anthony, 1979). In this way, the client system *owns* the course of action that is taken.

This is where cooking diverges from social work. For when we are preparing food, we are dealing with inanimate objects. Often, as the cook, we are the decision maker. However, we still have options, and the importance of the decision may be based on data we collect (availability of fresh ingredients, budget constraints, time available for cooking, number of people eating). Sometimes, it's helpful to cook or bake something that can serve an all-purpose need. Short dough, for example, can be used for many functions. It can be used as a base for a fruit bar, or as a pie crust, or stand alone as sugar cookies. It is up to you to make the decision about how to use the dough. Thus, one recipe can provide you with a variety of different outcomes depending on the situation.

Short Dough

1 lb sugar (2 cups)	5 oz water
1 tbsp salt	1 tbsp vanilla
⅓ cup corn syrup	2 lb flour (approx. 7 cups of all-purpose flour)
1 lb shortening (2 cups)	
3 eggs	1 tsp baking powder

Blend sugar, salt, corn syrup, and shortening until soft and smooth. Add the eggs in two stages and blend well. Stir in the water and vanilla. Add the flour and baking powder. Fold or mix lightly until the flour is absorbed. Do not overmix.

The dough should have a rough, uneven texture and appearance. It will be smoothed by using a floured cloth when you work the dough. If you are making the short dough for a pie crust, take a cloth and sprinkle flour on it. Place the dough on the cloth, and roll with a rolling pin. You can use 2 sheets of wax paper instead of the flour cloth. Sandwich the dough between the wax paper, and roll with a rolling pin. Refrigerate the dough to keep it firm.

Quick Short Dough Fruit Bars

Preheat the oven to 400 degrees. (Baking in a cool oven may cause the filling to boil over before the dough is baked.) Place the short dough in a cleaned and greased 9- x 12-inch pan. The bottom of the dough should be even. Fill the pan about three-fourths full with a fruit filling (one can of prepared fruit filling of your choice is sufficient). You can top the filling with a lattice top of the short dough if desired.

Bake until the dough is light brown (about 35 minutes). Let cool and cut into squares.

If you are making cookies from the short dough, cut them as regular sugar cookies and bake them on an ungreased cookie sheet at 400 degrees for 8 to 12 minutes.

Social work also involves some all-purpose skills. The skills of interviewing and active listening are the foundations of many different interventions. And there is some commonality to these skills regardless of the nature of the client system and/or the environment.

Evaluating Outcomes Leading to Termination

It is certainly important to know whether we were effective in our intervention. The question arises as to how to measure whether we were effective or not. As stated earlier, the systems perspective provides some guidance in looking at the difference between outputs and outcomes. But the question still arises as to how to monitor whether the output does align with the anticipated outcome. What techniques can be used to monitor the progress we are having with our client systems?

Linked with evaluation is the aspect of termination. For if we have successfully achieved a desired outcome, then it is appropriate to terminate the relationship so that the client doesn't become dependent on the social worker. There are four tasks that are part of a successful termination process (Hepworth, Rooney, & Larsen, 1997, p. 598):

1. Determine when to implement termination.
2. Mutually resolve emotional reactions experienced during the process of separation.
3. Evaluate the service provided and the extent to which goals were accomplished.
4. Provide a plan to maintain gains achieved and to achieve continued growth.

Evaluating outcomes has become a more prominent part of social work practice over the past 20 years. It is important to evaluate the effectiveness of our actions since learning what is or isn't effective helps to build additional scientific knowledge on how to address problems. Evaluation is linked to termination because it is important to determine if the termination is appropriate. There are three different areas or dimensions that need to be evaluated: the outcome, the process, and the practitioner (Hepworth, Rooney, & Larsen, 1997, p. 608). Obviously, it is important to determine whether the goals set by the client were achieved; however, if we are unable to identify the process that we took for that goal to be achieved, then we will be unable to replicate the process when a similar situation arises. In addition, the client will not have developed the skills to address a similar problem in the future. It is also important to assess our role as a practitioner. As part of our professional growth and development, it is important to continue on a path of self-inquiry. That path includes getting feedback about our effectiveness from our clients. Thus, evaluation is a little more complicated than just stating that goals were achieved.

There are many different techniques that are used to evaluate practice. Some of these are quantitative measures while others are qualitative. The nature of this text is not intended to explore these different techniques. In fact, there are courses offered within your curriculum that focus solely on this topic. It is important that you learn to integrate the content from those courses into your own practice so that you can evaluate your own effectiveness in working with actual client systems. Techniques are very individualized, and each client system also needs to be assessed as an individual. So, even though there are certain techniques that can be applied across the board, each one is modified by the individual social worker in response to the particular circumstances.

As an example, throughout this book there are references to cooking or baking times. For example, to tell whether the bread is done baking, I usually include a time followed by "or until the dough has a brown top and a bottom and the bread sounds hollow when tapped." Baking times are only approximations. There is still the individual aspect of looking at the product, touching it, smelling it, and hearing it to see if it is done. These steps are very important and are part of the individual choice of doneness. For example, some people think that I underbake my challah, but that is because I prefer that bread to melt in the mouth rather than have a hard crust. Thus, part of cooking involves relying on our senses and collecting information to determine whether what we have cooked is acceptable.

This is not to say that we can declare that we were successful because it "feels right." There still needs to be some scientific foundation that determines success. For example, the bread is done because it has a brown top and bottom and sounds hollow. We can also say that we were successful in an intervention with a client because the client expressed satisfaction with the intervention and no longer needs our services. We are still relying on our senses, but we gathered information through our senses and used that information to determine our success.

Sharing Knowledge and Technological Advances

Throughout this book and your course of study in social work you will continually discover that our level of knowledge is not 100 percent complete. Our theories do not fully explain situations in the real world, which leads to contradictions between what we observe and what we believe to be true. For example, we generally accept the theory of gravity that there is an attraction between objects and that the smaller object will be drawn to the larger object. So, if we drop something, it falls to the ground. We can anticipate the outcome based on the theory. However, the theories in the social sciences are not as reliable in predicting events. This means that social workers must constantly observe situations to try to understand the quality of the specific situation and determine whether it can be generalized to similar situations. This is how knowledge is built. As professionals, we have the responsibility to share new knowledge with colleagues through presentations at professional meetings and publication in professional journals and books. The sharing of knowledge makes possible technological advances in the field and improves our effectiveness. That is why it's important to continually read and understand how the technology can be used to answer the questions that constantly arise in the field.

This constant sense of discovery and technological advances applies to all fields, not just social work. For example, I recently stumbled on an old tool that can be used as a technological advance. Have you ever tried to peel garlic? Garlic has a papery skin around each clove that is a problem to remove. There are plenty of devices on the market that claim to be garlic peelers and cost a lot of money. What I discovered is that I could use a flat rubber jar opener to peel the garlic clove. (These jar openers are usually handed out free at exhibits by different companies as advertisements.) You take the garlic clove and place it in the middle of the jar opener and then wrap the jar opener around it. Then you place the rolled up jar opener between your hands and rub your hands together gently. Off comes the garlic paper.

Critical Thinking Prompts

- Go back through the chapter and see if you can arrive at your own metaphors for each of the different sections: conscious use of self, defining issues, collecting and assessing data, planning and contracting, using the problem-solving process, identifying alternative interventions, selecting and implementing appropriate courses of action, evaluating outcomes and sharing knowledge and technological advances.

- Identify those skills that you feel are important in working with people. Develop a mechanism for explaining these skills to people other than social workers.

- Think about a situation and develop some strategies for assessing if you were effective in the intervention that you set out to do.

CHAPTER 5

Social Welfare Policy

WHAT'S IN THIS CHAPTER:

- Description of social welfare policy as a transfer of resources
- Discussion of economic factors
- Description of the interplay between history and values as it relates to social work practice
- Discussion of the effect of policy on social work practice

Throughout this text I have talked about the ecological systems perspective as an organizing framework within social work practice. By using this framework, social work teaches that "all systems exist as part of an *ecosystem*—a set of interconnected, interdependent, and interactive systems that affect one another" (Miley, O'Melia, & DuBois, 1998, p. 48). To fully understand one system, one must look at it within the context of the other systems that are interacting with it. These other systems are not always equal. Sometimes there are systems that incorporate others or sometimes one system may be affected by many other systems.

Client System as Part of Supra System

To simplify, and bring the concept down to the human level, there are those individuals who have resources and those who do not. Societies often create mechanisms that transfer resources from those who have to those who do not (Chatterjee, 1996). This transfer of resources is referred to as social services (Karger & Stoesz, 1998). Social services exist in a society to promote the welfare of that society's citizenry. Social policy involves the rules and regulations that dictate how that welfare is defined within that society.

Social policy can be defined as a set of rules established by a governing body that addresses the needs of the people being served. From a public policy perspective, countries adopt the "right" policies to achieve the "right" goals (Dye, 1987, p. 5). As social workers it is important to understand how our country defines "right," as that will help us better understand the factors that affect our clients and the resources we will have to help them. This information is part of the policy analysis process in social work education.

For example, a woman on AFDC used her first check to buy a waterbed. The social worker wondered why she used that money to buy a waterbed when she had other needs, like paying the rent. The worker soon realized that this was the largest amount of money that the woman had ever received at one time and no one had ever helped her with budgeting. Add to this the materialistic values of our society, and it makes sense that she would buy something for herself rather than taking care of responsibilities.

I experienced a similar value conflict when I worked in public housing. I was amazed at how few people there had phones in their homes; to try to reach them by phone I had to call a neighbor. These same residents had cable television. Sure, the cable company had offered free hookups to everyone in the housing project. But it seemed a conflict in values when residents chose cable television over telephones. Again, it was important to understand the client system within the larger ecological environment.

Policy as Part of the Interplay Between History and Values

In order to look at policy as a system, it is important to understand some of the components that make up that policy. Dye (1987, p. 6) states that there are three interconnected components of the policy system: current social and economic conditions within society; institutions, processes, and behaviors of the political system to address these conditions; and current public policies. I would add that these need to be looked at within the context of the historical development of that society and the values of that society. By looking at these five aspects of a policy system it is possible to begin to develop a strategy to analyze policy and look at how it affects particular client systems.

Within social work, the term *policy* refers to more than just the study of public policy, although public policy is an important aspect of social work. The United States consists of "a pluralistic mix of private and public services" (Karger & Stoesz, 1998, p. 2). So we need to look at all policies, rules, and societal values that affect our clients, either directly or indirectly.

The Council on Social Work Education Curriculum Policy Statement (1994) dictates the nature of the social welfare policy curriculum for accredited social work programs. The CPS states, "Social welfare policy and services content must include the history, mission, and philosophy of the social work profession.

Content must be presented about the history and current patterns of provisions of social welfare services, the role of social policy in helping or deterring people in the maintenance or attainment of optimal health and well-being, and the effect of policy on social work practice" (pp. 102, 141).

Another way of stating this is that policy helps us understand the larger context, both from a historical perspective and from looking at the rules and regulations that dictate the structure of the social environment and their effects on client systems.

Transfer of Resources

Let's try to understand some of the larger social factors that govern our social system. First are economic factors. Economic factors basically involve the purchase of goods and services—in other words, how we meet our basic needs. In our society, we believe that some minimal standard of living should exist for all citizens. One way to provide this standard involves transferring resources from those who have to those who do not have. Understanding the policies that dictate how much resources are transferred becomes an important part of understanding the values of our society.

It is important to understand the relationship between policies and economic transfers. For example, social welfare policy began in Germany at the end of nineteenth century as a result of worker unrest. Bismarck created labor policies to quiet the masses in order to maintain control of the government. In the United States, Social Security was instituted in 1935 as part of the New Deal to quiet the elderly and the great number of unemployed persons. Prior to that time, the United States maintained an individualistic value system that relied on fending for oneself. The Social Security Act was contrary to that value because it meant the government would take some responsibility for care of the aged, war survivors, and the disabled.

Since Social Security was enacted in 1935, critics have argued that the government has taken too much leeway in caring for its citizens. The struggle between government intervention and individual rights is an ongoing battle. That battle exists because of the ethical conflict of social versus individual responsibilities.

As social workers, we have the responsibility to be aware of social and government policies and how they affect our client systems. Within Maslow's hierarchy of needs people should think of obtaining shelter prior to the purchase of a waterbed. However, if an individual still chooses to buy the waterbed first, then that is legally allowed, although the individual must bear the consequences of that behavior. Thus, social policies do affect the individual in an indirect way.

Economic factors obviously affect what we cook or bake. Have you ever gone to a grocery store and been shocked by the prices? For example, walk down the cereal aisle of a store. You'll see name brand and generic brand cereals. Usually the name brand will be much more expensive than the generic or store brand. Does that mean that it's better? Would you buy it because of name recognition or because you know it's a better product? Some people buy the name brand at its higher price because they recognize the name—which is why there is so much advertising of name brands. Others may buy both, sample them, and thereafter buy the brand whose taste they prefer. Others may judge the cereals solely on price, and always buy the cheaper item. Sometimes economics is the main determinant, sometimes it's just one of the factors. But, for most of us, economics enters into all of our decisions.

Economics does not just mean dollars and cents. Time is also an economic factor. Both time and money are involved in our meal decisions.

Consider, for a moment, the "lowly" bean. Beans are probably one of the most misunderstood foods. They have been classified as peasant food, only to be eaten when meat is unavailable or unaffordable. Yet beans are one of the most nutritious foods available and provide some of the best health benefits for people. "Beans are superior to bread, cereals, potatoes, and pasta as a source of carbohydrates for diabetics and joggers. They are an excellent source of dietary fiber (promoting regularity and keeping colon cancer at bay). They help control blood cholesterol and blood glucose while being free of cholesterol themselves. They help control weight by retaining water in the digestive tract, thus promoting a feeling of fullness and delaying the return of hunger" (Stone & Stone, 1988, p. 3). Beans are also an excellent source of protein. With all these benefits, let's try preparing some healthy, filling dishes using beans—one way to address economic concerns.

If you are also concerned about the economics of time, you can use canned beans. In canned beans the beans have already been soaked and cooked. Canned beans cost about 30 cents more a pound than dry beans, but there is the convenience of opening the can and using it right away rather than letting the beans soak overnight and having to cook them for 2 hours to make them tender.

Black Beans and Rice (Frijoles Negroes con Arroz)

1 lb dry black beans (2 cups)	2 pieces of sun-dried toma-
6 cups water	toes (optional)
1 vegetable bouillon cube	2 carrots, sliced (optional)
1 large chopped onion	3 tbsp extra virgin olive oil
2 bay leaves	2 jalapeño peppers (optional)
2 garlic cloves, chopped	1 tbsp cumin
(optional)	salt and pepper to taste

In a large pot, soak the beans in cold water overnight or for at least 8 hours. Pour out the water (this removes much of the gas associated with eating beans), and place the beans, water, bouillon cube, and bay leaves in a 4-quart pot. Bring to a boil and then turn the heat down to low. Heat the oil in a skillet and sauté the onions and garlic. Add them and the other vegetables to the cooking beans. Cook for about 2 hours or until the beans are tender, stirring occasionally. Add the cumin, salt, and pepper. Serve over rice (see recipe in Chapter 4). Serves 6. Refrigerate leftovers; reheat and eat them within 5 days. Leftovers may also be frozen, then defrosted and reheated.

Vegetarian Black Bean Chili

The above recipe can be modified to make a vegetarian black bean chili. Reduce the water to 3 cups and add a can of Italian plum tomatoes (35 ounces) with the liquid. In addition, add 1 small seeded pasilla chili pepper, ½ teaspoon cayenne pepper, 1 tablespoon oregano, 1 dried chipotle chile pepper, 1 seeded green pepper, and ½ tablespoon dried cilantro to the cooking bean mixture.

Pasta is another food that helps ease economic conditions. It is low in fat and provides a nutritious meal that can be served elegantly. The calories derive from the different sauces that are added to the pasta, not from the pasta itself. Below is a very simple pasta dish that adds pizzazz to a meal during the week.

Pasta and Garlic

1 lb of your favorite pasta

½ cup extra virgin olive oil

4 garlic cloves (chopped)

½ chopped medium onion (optional)

3 pieces of sun-dried tomatoes

8 oz frozen mixed vegetables

2 tsp basil

salt and pepper to taste

Cook your favorite pasta following the directions on the package. Sauté the garlic, onions, and sun-dried tomatoes in the olive oil. Defrost the frozen vegetables by rinsing them in warm water or add them frozen to the boiling pasta in the last 3 minutes of cooking time. Mix all the ingredients together. The dish may be served either hot or cold. Serves 4.

As you can see, these recipes do not have any meat in them. Meat can be added; however, if a family is on a tight budget and is trying to make every dollar count, it is possible to prepare these inexpensive, elegant meals without meat.

The History and Current Patterns of Provisions of Social Welfare

The U.S. concept of social welfare emerged from the English Poor Laws of 1601 (Day, 1997). Yet the two systems are quite different because of their underlying different value orientations. The U.S. system is based on middle-class values whereas the British system emerged more from a colonial administration value system (Chatterjee, 1996). In the middle-class value orientation, individualistic methods are more valued; a person can move from the lower class to the middle class as a result of hard work. The colonial value system, in contrast, segregates the social classes and assumes that the upper class will care for the lower class.

A good analogy of how differences can affect policy can be made with gefilte fish. This is a Jewish fish dish that was developed from the common fish of the area. There is no such fish as a gefilte; however, poor Jews in Europe would take buffalo fish or carp and grind it with eggs, matzah meal, carrots, and onions and then cook it to make gefilte fish. When Jews came to the United States, they found areas where other fish were more common than buffalo fish. So, Jews around the Great Lakes make gefilte fish with pike and whitefish, whereas Jews in Vancouver make gefilte fish with salmon.

Gefilte Fish

3 lb pike	3 eggs
3 lb whitefish	3/4 cup ice water
5 onions	½ tsp of sugar (more can be added to taste)
2 quarts of water	
4 tsp salt	3 tbsp matzah meal
1½ tsp pepper	3 carrots

Fillet the fish and reserve the skin, heads, and bones. Combine head, skin, bones, with 4 sliced onions in 1 quart of water. Add 2 teaspoons salt and ¾ teaspoon pepper. Cook over high heat while preparing the fish.

Grind the fish (in a food processor, or have the fish market grind it for you) and the remaining onions (a carrot could
also be added). Place in a chopping bowl and add the eggs,
water, sugar, matzah meal, and remaining salt and pepper.
Chop until very fine—this is important for fluffy fish. Moisten
your hands and shape the mixture into balls. Carefully drop
the balls into the fish stock. Add the carrots. Cover loosely
and cook over low heat for 1½ hours. Remove the cover for
the last ½ hour. Taste to correct seasoning. Cool the fish
balls slightly before removing them to a bowl or platter.
Strain the stock over the gefilte fish, and arrange carrots
around the pieces. Chill. Serve with horseradish.
Serves 12 people generously.

As we have learned, social work follows a problem-solving
process. Social welfare policy also follows a problem-solving process. But while, policy usually emerges in response to a problem,
it is not a simple relationship and not all problems generate social
welfare policies (Karger & Stoesz, 1998, p. 4). The complication
arises because of the interplay of values relating to the social policies. For one example, when the Social Security Act was passed in
1935, there was no provision for health coverage. This was a result
of the feeling that health insurance should remain a separate en-
tity. However, 30 years later, Medicaid became part of the War on
Poverty legislation, and medical coverage became an entitlement
for the poor (Schorr, 1986). (Entitlement is the services, goods, or
money due to an individual by virtue of a specific status [Barker,
1995, p. 121].) Current events and the interplay between economic factors and the values of the society will continue to influence social welfare policies.

The Effect of Policy on Social Work Practice

As values in a society change, so does policy, and changes in
policy affect social work practice. As an example, in 1992 Gover-
nor John Engler made Michigan the first state in the union to

eliminate general assistance benefits. General assistance is a cash grant program where money goes directly to poor single adults. The state of Michigan's Department of Social Services was able to reduce its budget as a result of this move. However, the effect of this change was also to increase the numbers of people using shelters and going to soup kitchens. In other words, the ramifications of policy changes will be felt in many aspects of society. As social workers, it is important for us to understand how policy changes will affect our client systems.

Food preparation is pretty similar. If we change an ingredient in a recipe, it affects other aspects of the recipe. Sometimes the change will be good (as in budget savings by eliminating general assistance), and sometimes the change will cause problems in other areas (as in the added drain on homeless shelters and soup kitchens caused by the elimination of general assistance). If you are looking for consistency, then don't change the recipe. However, there will be times when you either want to change the recipe or need to change the recipe. In either case, remember that there will be a change in the outcome.

It is like making rugelach, a cream-cheese-dough pastry. You may know some people who are lactose intolerant or who do not want a dairy pastry. A soy-based cream cheese is available on the market; and for people who want low fat, there is a low fat cream cheese on the market. In either case, using either the soy cream cheese or the low fat cream cheese will change the outcome. The soy cream cheese has a salty taste while the low fat cream cheese is softer and more liquid. Thus changing that one ingredient provides positives in one area but those need to be compensated as a result of the change in ingredient.

Rugelach

I lb cream cheese	I lb flour
I lb margarine	I tsp vanilla
12 oz confectioners' sugar	pinch of baking powder

Blend the cream cheese in a mixer until it is medium hard and plastic. Do the same with the margarine. Then blend the two together. Add the sugar, flour, and vanilla and blend. Add the flour at slow speed and blend until smooth.

Place the dough on the table and form a rectangle. Allow it to rest for 10 minutes, then roll it out, fold, and refrigerate. Repeat this procedure two more times. Cover the dough after the final roll and refrigerate it overnight or for several hours. This will allow the dough to condition.

After it is conditioned, roll out the dough to about ⅛-inch thickness. Wash the dough with melted margarine, sprinkle it with raisins, nuts, cake crumbs, cinnamon-sugar, or whatever filling you want. Then lightly roll the filling into the dough with gentle pressure. Cut the dough into pieces about 1 inch wide and 2 inches long. Roll them and place them on a greased, shallow pan. Allow them to rest on the pan about ½ hour before baking.

Bake in a 350-degree oven until they are light brown and crisp.

Critical Thinking Prompts

- Provide your own metaphor to explain the transfer of goods and services of the social welfare system.

- Identify some cost-saving measures you could incorporate into your life without sacrificing the quality of that life.

- Describe the values that have influenced your life and the way you interact with others.

- Identify different systems that encompass your environment. Can you identify the policies that govern those various systems? How many of them are public and how many are private?

CHAPTER 6

Field Practicum

WHAT'S IN THIS CHAPTER:

- Definition of field practicum
- Description of different people in the field experience

An integral part of social work education is the field experience or practicum. The practicum is where you, as the student, "learn how to do it: how to apply theoretical social work material to a hands-on situation; how to cope with the practical limitations of a real life environment; how to be useful to real people with real problems in a real setting that is less than ideal" (Collins, Thomlison, & Grinnell, 1992, p. 1). The practicum experience gives you the opportunity to integrate the information and theories that you learned in the classroom with real-life experiences. The CSWE Curriculum Policy Statement (1994) states: "The field practicum is an integral component of the curriculum in social work education. It engages the student in supervised social work practice and provides opportunities to apply classroom learning in the field setting" (pp. 102, 142).

The field practicum is a transition between class and practice. It is your opportunity to test the things you have learned in class in a practice setting. Because it is still a class, you can make mistakes since you are supervised by the program and the agency. You will have a field instructor, the agency representative who will supervise your field experience, and a faculty advisor or liaison between the social work program and the agency. The faculty advisor's responsibility is to work with you and the field instructor to ensure that you are gaining a social work experience that conforms to the mission and goals of the social work program. Thus, as a student, your role is to have the opportunity to experience social work as a profession, learn from the experience, and refine your skills before you enter the profession as a beginning social worker. This scenario is like an appetizer to a meal, since the purpose of the appetizer is to give one a sense of eating before participating in the full meal.

Just as the field practicum is like an appetizer to the profession, it is useful to have appetizers for some meals. An easy appetizer to prepare is jalapeño cream cheese roll-ups. They can be used as finger food at a party or before a meal or as a snack after dinner. Remember, appetizers are not full meals but only provide a taste of a meal. The field practicum is your taste of the profession.

Jalapeño Cream Cheese Roll-Ups

8-oz package cream cheese

1 oz chopped jalapeño peppers (use more or less depending on your taste)

1 package flour tortilla shells (usually 8 to 12 in a package)

1 jar salsa (use whatever prepared salsa you like or make your own)

Thoroughly mix the chopped jalapeños and the cream cheese in a bowl. Thinly spread the cream cheese mixture on a tortilla shell so that one side is completely covered. Roll the tortilla shell with the cream cheese mixture on the inside so the tortilla shell looks like a cigar. Spread the remaining tortilla shells with the cream cheese and roll them. Wrap the roll-ups in foil and refrigerate them until ready to use. Place salsa in a bowl, cut the cigar-shaped tortilla shells into 2-inch tubes, and serve.

Some programs offer concurrent field and classroom experiences while others provide the field practicum after all the course content has been completed. Regardless of the model, each program utilizes a combination of people in partnership to ensure the educational experience of the student. Each member of the partnership plays an important role. "Most social work programs place the major responsibility for the integration of classroom learning and field instruction on the faculty field liaison" (Royse, Dhooper, & Rompf, 1993, p. 8). It is the faculty liaison's responsibility to make sure that the field experience is consistent with the social work educational experience presented by the program. There are a number of tools that the liaison can use. These include learning plans or contracts and process recordings.

We already looked at contracts in Chapter 4. Now you apply the elements of contracting you learned in the classroom by doing contracting with yourself as the client to develop a contract of learning goals within the agency setting (Friedman & Neuman, 1997). The liaison will monitor the contract to make sure that it is consistent with the social work curriculum.

Process recordings are another tool that the liaison may use. A process record is an accounting of a specific interaction between the social worker (in this case, the student) and the client. Here the student presents an incident in written form and assesses what transpired, including looking at his or her own gut-level feelings about the event and interpreting those feelings. The field instructor (agency staff) puts in supervisory comments. The faculty liaison can use the process record as a tool to identify the growth patterns of the student and the appropriateness of the interactions (Neuman & Friedman, 1997).

From this brief discussion it is possible to see that each person involved in the field practicum plays an important role in the student's learning process. That is why field practicums are partnerships between programs and agencies.

There are a lot of foods that relate to the concept of partnership: ice cream and cake at a birthday party, pancakes and syrup in the morning, macaroni and cheese at lunch. What a partnership infers is that there are at least two separate entities that are fine by themselves but better when combined. The field relationship is very much like that. Without the relationship, the program and the agency will do all right. However, the partnership enhances the experiences for all involved. The faculty liaison's experience is enhanced because she or he is provided a direct link to the field. The field instructor's experience is enhanced because the contact helps him or her remain current with the literature and new findings in the academic world. It also forces the field instructor to translate secondary thinking processes (those things that have become second nature in practice) into words that can be transmitted to the student. And the student benefits because the partnership provides an experience that integrates the content from the classroom into life experiences.

One can think of the field partnership as a smoothie. A smoothie is a blended drink with the basic ingredients being ice and fruit. Each is good on its own, but the partnering of these ingredients creates a nutritious, low-fat beverage, filled with vitamins.

Strawberry Banana Smoothie

1½ cups shaved ice (shaved ice provides a better
   consistency to the drink)

¾ cup strawberries

½ cup banana (1 banana)

1½ tbsp turbinado (raw sugar, or any sugar or
   sugar substitute)

2½ tbsp coconut milk

½ cup skim milk

Place all ingredients in a blender and blend until smooth (about 1 minute). Yield: 16 oz.

Critical Thinking Prompts

- Use your own metaphor to define the field practicum.
- Find a metaphor for each of the members of the partnership in the field experience.
- Identify three other types of partnerships that exist in life.

CHAPTER 7

Cultural Diversity

WHAT'S IN THIS CHAPTER:

- Definition of cultural diversity
- Discussion of similarities and differences among cultures

The United States came into existence as a haven for immigrants seeking to escape oppression. And many people of many different cultures have come and are still coming to the United States. All of these people have had to learn to work and coexist together. One of the roles of social work is to help with the integration of these different cultures. So it is fitting that the social work profession has its roots in the United States.

Cultural Diversity Defined

Cultural diversity has become something of a buzz phrase within social work. It refers to the fact that there are so many different cultures and no majority culture in the United States, which creates cultural pluralism. Barker (1995) defines cultural pluralism as "the existence within a society of various racial, religious, and ethnic groups, as well as other distinct groups, each of which has different values and lifestyles" (p. 87). Cultural diversity or cultural pluralism is important within social work for two reasons. First, from an ecological systems perspective, it is important to recognize how the interaction of each of these different cultures affects each person within our society. This is done on a macro level, as in looking at the interaction between cultural groups; on a mezzo level, as in looking at the influence that the group has on its members; and, finally, on a micro level, by looking at the effect that the culture has on each individual.

Second, culture diversity is important because of one of the values of social work, self-determination. Self-determination means that each person has the right to determine her or his own destiny and make her or his own choices. This is where theory and values intersect with actions. The way a person makes choices and decisions is heavily based on that person's value orientation. That value orientation is influenced by his or her culture. Of course, this is a very simplified description of cultural diversity, but awareness of cultural diversity has become an important component within social work education in order to help professionals gain skills in working with people from diverse backgrounds, especially backgrounds that are different from their own.

Acceptance of Others

A basic tenet in social work practice is for the professional to be able to accept other people as they are. In other words, we need to be able to recognize and accept differences among people and cultures. However, in order to accept those differences it is important to first understand and accept oneself. Accepting oneself involves an introspective look at those factors and characteristics that contribute to one's behaviors and actions. Many times these have been influenced by stories our parents told us as we were growing up or by other subtle experiences that we had by being part of a cultural group. Development of self also emerges from such cultural factors as gender, race, religion, and parents' country or countries of origin. Various combinations of these experiences contribute to each individual's definition of self.

The Council of Social Work Education's Curriculum Policy Statement (1994) states: "Professional social work education is committed to preparing students to understand and appreciate human diversity. Programs must provide curriculum content about differences and similarities in the experiences, needs, and beliefs of people. . . . These include, but are not limited to groups distinguished by race, ethnicity, culture, class, gender, sexual orientation, religion, physical or mental disability, age, and national origin" (pp. 101, 140).

The CPS is all encompassing, mentioning various aspects of our society. Devore and Schlesinger (1991) state that there was little mobility between groups prior to industrialization and modernization. However, massive industrialization and urbanization gave rise to diverse bases of identity (p. 21). Whereas ethnicity used to be confined to segregated areas, now ethnicities mix. Since ethnicity as a basis for one's identity continues to be strong, it is important to learn about the similarities and differences among people in order to be a more effective social worker.

The food we eat is strongly affected by the culture we were brought up in and the larger culture/society we live in. For example, I had an aunt who used to burn everything (this was before blackened food became popular). My cousins used to think that a fried egg was a blackened egg. That was their culture within their household. But cultures also embrace different foods. Often these different foods are so incorporated into the larger society that we think of them as "American." Think of egg rolls and chow mein (Chinese origins), spaghetti (Italian by way of China), hot dogs (German), wraps (a form of burrito from Mexico)—the list could go on and on. Thus, we need to look at what we can learn from other cultures and bring that knowledge into our own culture.

Just as diversity exists throughout our culture, this book, and the social work profession, diversity exists in the foods we eat. Consider the recipe below. The dish is sometimes called an Italian omelet. Although its origin is in Italy, many people think of it as a Mexican dish. And we are now cooking it in the United States—despite our different backgrounds.

Frittata

Frittata, or Italian omelet, is a delicious egg dish that can be served as a main course.

2 to 3 small red potatoes	4 oz feta cheese
1 medium onion	3 tbsp margarine or olive oil
2 garlic cloves, minced	2 tbsp cilantro (fresh or dried)
½ red bell pepper	
½ green bell pepper	salt and pepper to taste
8 eggs	

Thinly slice the small red potatoes and boil them in water for 10 minutes. While the potatoes are cooking, sauté the onions and garlic in the margarine or olive oil at low to medium heat in a 10-inch skillet. Chop the peppers and add them to the onion-garlic mixture. Drain the potatoes and add them to the onion-garlic-pepper mixture. Continue sautéing over a low to medium heat. Whip the eggs. Crumble the feta cheese over the vegetable mixture. Add the cilantro to the whipped eggs, add salt and pepper to taste, and then pour the eggs over the vegetables. Turn the heat down to low and cover the pan. Cook until the eggs are firm. (If the bottom is set but the top still needs more time, you may want to put the pan under the broiler.) Invert the frittata onto a serving plate and cut it into wedges. Serve it hot or at room temperature. Serves 6 to 8.

Similarities and Differences

One culture can borrow many things from another, and an experience may be similar in different cultures but given a different name in each. For example, Italians use the term ravioli to refer to a filled noodle, Chinese refer to it as won ton, and Jews as kreplach. Each filled noodle is slightly different, both in shape and fillings, yet each is still a "filled noodle." For example, all cultures have "families," yet the makeup of the families may differ as may the expectations of behavior for different members.

There are, of course, many things that vary slightly from one culture to the other. Food is certainly one of these things. As noted, similar items are used in different cultures. How the culture uses the item is different. Consider, for example, the cucumber. Cucumbers can be pickled or cut up fresh into salads. Below is a cucumber dish that will bring some cultural diversity into your life.

Egyptian Cucumber and Onion Salad

3 cucumbers	3 tbsp lemon juice
3 small onions	3 tbsp extra virgin olive oil
4 oz feta cheese	salt and pepper to taste

Slice the cucumbers and onions and arrange them on a serving dish. In a blender or food processor, mix the feta cheese, lemon juice, olive oil, salt, and pepper until smooth. Pour over the sliced cucumbers and onions and serve. Serves 8.

Critical Thinking Prompts

- Identify the source of origin for the foods you eat during a week.
- Describe yourself in ethnic terms. Use the categories of race, gender, sexual orientation, and so on that the CSWE CPS uses.
- How is your life affected by other cultures?
- Are your friends from different cultures? Name the cultures.

Populations at Risk

ccording to the National Association of Social Workers (NASW), "The primary mission of the social work profession is to enhance human well-being and help meet basic human needs, with particular attention to the needs of vulnerable, oppressed, and poor people" (quoted in Hepworth, Rooney, & Larsen, 1997, p. 4). How do we define vulnerable, oppressed, and poor people? A general term is *populations at risk*. This is defined as "those members of a group who are vulnerable to, or likely to be harmed by, a specific medical, social, or environmental circumstance" (Barker, 1995, p. 28). Another way to look at these populations or social systems is as those who "are vulnerable to specific problems, although such problems have yet to surface. In other words, identifiable conditions exist that predict a negative impact on social functioning" (DuBois & Miley, 1996, p. 67). These definitions still do not define clear parameters for at-risk populations; however, they provide guidelines within which the profession operates in defining whom we serve.

The Council on Social Work Education also takes a stand at translating these definitions into a curricular position to be incorporated into social work education. According to the Curriculum Policy Statement, social work education should include

> content about patterns, dynamics, and consequences of discrimination, economic deprivation, and oppression. The curriculum must provide content about people of color, women, and gay and lesbian persons. Such content must emphasize the impact of discrimination, economic deprivation, and oppression upon these groups . . . In addition to those mandated above, such groups include, but are not limited to, those distinguished by age, ethnicity, culture, class, religion, and physical or mental disability. (Council on Social Work Education, 1994, pp. 101, 140)

Thus, discrimination, economic deprivation, and oppression are contributing factors that lead to populations being at risk. Because the mission of social work is to enhance human well-being, it is the role of the social worker to address the needs of populations at risk. Within the social work curriculum, one would define a population at risk by focusing on a particular population and describing how factors of discrimination, economic deprivation, and oppression relate to that population and place it at risk.

Institutional Factors

The emphasis in the social work curriculum is on how the differences of a group lead that group to be discriminated against, or face economic deprivation and/or oppression within the larger society. For example, a significant number of people of color have never attended college. We, as social workers, need to ask what was the rationale for not attending college. It could be that they did not have the opportunity because outside forces (poverty, poor schools) prevented them from attending or it could be that as a group they lacked a frame of reference for attending college. For example, consider an actual project to work with at-risk, minority high school students to help them realize their academic potential. I worked on such a project in which there was a participant, named Valerie, who grew up in a household where multiple generations had been on welfare. She was the first member of her family to even be close to graduating from high school, let alone attending college. Yet her frame of reference was to consider a vocational/technical program after high school graduation to learn to be a medical assistant rather than think about the possibility of attending medical school, although she had the capability (Friedman, 1997). The effect of the discrimination that her family faced over the years put her at risk of not achieving her potential.

The Social Work Process

The social work curriculum focuses on understanding patterns that discrimination has created over the years. These patterns become ingrained into the person's thinking and behavior processes, affecting the way that society and opportunities are viewed. In Valerie's case, the experience of multiple generations on welfare did not provide any perspective for attending college. Her frame of reference was to graduate from high school, get some professional training, and then get a job as quickly as possible. So, even though she had taken steps beyond her family's experience, her perspective was still limited.

Another example is the Jewish community. Many members of the Jewish community have been able to achieve levels of economic success. However, the Jewish liturgy continues to emphasize those historical events that have led to hardships for Jews. There are references to being slaves in Egypt and to realizing the impact of slavery on one's life. So although many Jews have never personally experienced slavery, it is paramount within their existence and their tradition. As a community Jews may not be perceived as suffering any economic deprivation. However, the emphasis in the community to maintain a separate identity does lead to potential discrimination and oppression.

In the United States there is a conflict between trying to "Americanize" all immigrants to one language and culture and accepting the differences among cultures (Iglehart & Becerra, 1995). As a society attempts to strive for a one language and culture perspective, it tends to discriminate against those who are different. By understanding the patterns, dynamics, and consequences of discrimination, economic deprivation, and oppression, social workers are better able to effect changes in society.

As social workers whose mission is to enhance the well-being of our clients, we also need to understand the consequences of the role of power in society. We must also be aware of how power affects our role with our clients. Day (1997, p. 2) describes two functions in social welfare: social control and social treatment. She states that there is a very fine line between whether we are actually providing treatment or asserting a form of social control. As we look at our role in the helping field, it is important to understand the dynamics between control and treatment so that we are actually providing treatment.

For example, as social workers we have the duty to report suspected child abuse cases. The underlying premise to this duty is that by reporting the case to Child Protective Services (CPS) we ensure that the child will be protected and the family will receive treatment. A dilemma can occur when we deal with other cultures. I serve on the board of directors of an agency specializing in providing shelter and services for people seeking asylum in the United States or Canada. Clients from all over the world come to Freedom House to escape the discrimination that they faced in their countries of origin. Many times, these refugees have left family and friends behind, and they do not know anyone in their new country.

In this example a Pakistani family had arrived at Freedom House and was about two weeks away from receiving entry into Canada. The shelter is very crowded, and each family sleeps in one room until asylum is granted. During this one incident, the thirteen-year-old daughter reported to a nun at the local church that her father had hit her. The nun then contacted the agency to report it to CPS. The Freedom House staff faced a dilemma. If the staff reported the case to CPS, then it would surely hinder the family's chances for entry into Canada and might even precipitate deportation back to Pakistan. However, the family had escaped Pakistan because of religious discrimination and would almost certainly be executed upon return. Thus, the issue of treatment versus control in this case could mean life or death.

Discriminating between social control and social treatment is rather like making a quiche. The foundation of all quiches is pie crust. You can buy a prepared pie crust, but it is usually designed to fit an 8-inch pie pan rather than a quiche pan. It's easy enough to make your own quiche crust. Remember not to overwork the dough. Overworking the dough causes it to crumble rather than to form the proper consistency. Too much flour will dry out the dough. Not refrigerating the dough long enough or too long will either cause it to not set up properly or to dry out. Thus, in making your crust, it is important to understand the difference between treatment (making it with concern for its quality) versus control (forcing it to be something it is not ready to be).

Basic Quiche Crust

1 ¼ cups flour	3 tbsp shortening
pinch of salt	3 to 4 tbsp cold water
3 tbsp butter	

Blend the flour, salt, shortening, and butter with either a pastry blender or two knives. Once the dough is mixed and crumbly, add the water, 1 tablespoon at a time. Mix the water into the dough. You have used enough water when the dough is smooth and can be blended together into a ball. Refrigerate the dough for 1 hour. After refrigerating, roll the dough on a lightly floured cloth or between two sheets of lightly floured waxed paper. Roll to about ¼ or ⅛ inch thick. Place in quiche pan (or pie pan) and prick the bottom with a fork (this will permit air to escape as the dough bakes). Bake in a hot oven (450 degrees) for 10 minutes. Take the pan out of the oven and let the crust cool.

You can then fill your quiche with whatever filling you like. I personally like to take a small package of frozen spinach (about 8 ounces), thaw it, drain the water, and put it in the baked crust. I then put in chopped onions (to taste), about 6 ounces of grated cheese, and whatever seasoning I desire (usually a little salt and pepper). Then I add the custard.

Basic Quiche Custard

4 eggs

1½ cups cream

2 tbsp melted butter

1 tbsp flour

pinch salt

pinch cayenne pepper

pinch nutmeg

Mix all the ingredients together and pour them into the quiche crust. Bake in a moderate oven (375 degrees) for 35 to 45 minutes. The quiche is done when set with a slightly browned top. Serves 8.

Critical Thinking Prompts

- Define the concepts of discrimination, economic deprivation, and oppression in your own words or by using metaphors.
- How do discrimination, economic deprivation, and/or oppression contribute to a specific group being at risk?
- Describe what being at risk means to you.
- Describe in your own words the difference between controlling someone and providing treatment. Can you give a specific example of the difference?

CHAPTER 9

Social and Economic Justice

WHAT'S IN THIS CHAPTER:

- Definition of social justice

- Description of the relationship between social justice and the social work profession

- Discussion of how to operationalize social justice within social work

Throughout this text we have noted that the mission of social work "is to enhance human well-being and help meet basic human needs, with particular attention to the needs of vulnerable, oppressed, and poor people" (Hepworth, Rooney, & Larsen, 1997, p. 4). This belief arises from the belief "that society can be made wholesome by the application of scientific principles applied with love and kindness" (Specht & Courtney, 1994, p. 20). The profession has moved in two directions in defining these principles of love and kindness. One has been focusing on making society wholesome by working with individuals (an emphasis that emerged from the Charitable Organization Society movement and Mary Richmond), and the other focus has been on working with communities (an emphasis that emerged from the settlement house movement and Jane Addams) (Specht & Courtney, 1994, pp. 73, 80).

How each society develops and implements these principles of love and kindness is related to the values of social and economic justice. In our society, some goods and services are transferred from those people who have to those who do not. This transfer is called social welfare, and the professionals responsible for the transfer are social workers.

Defining Social Justice in Social Work

Social justice is defined as "an ideal condition in which all members of a society have the same basic rights, protections, opportunities, obligations, and social benefits" (Barker, 1995, p. 354). Adding the term *economic* to *social justice* expands the definition to include the right of people within society to have access to those items that will provide their basic needs, leading to the wholesomeness of a society.

The Curriculum Policy Statement of the Council on Social Work Education (1994) declares that

social work education must provide an understanding of the dynamics and consequences of social and economic injustice, including all forms of human oppression and discrimination. They must provide students with the skills to promote social change and to implement a wide range of interventions that further the achievement of individual and collective social and economic justice. Theoretical and practice content must be provided about strategies of intervention for achieving social and economic justice and for combating the causes and effects of institutionalized forms of oppression. (pp. 101, 140)

This curricular statement says a lot about the values of the social work profession and yet it is difficult to specifically operationalize. Since the content relates to basic foundations within the profession, many programs tend to integrate this content into existing curricular structures. But this does not answer how to operationalize this content, how to put it into practice.

Practicing Social Justice in Social Work

As social workers we are constantly faced with choices that relate to potential conflicts between the values of our client systems and those of the agency or larger social system. It becomes our responsibility to assess the situation and then help to make an appropriate response based on the knowledge at hand. For example, an underlying premise in the United States is that a client has the right to self-determination. This holds true for individuals, families, groups, and communities. Sometimes client self-determination is contrary to the policies of the social work agency, and the social worker must work to resolve the differences. The deciding factor in such a situation is what will work toward change that ameliorates oppression and discrimination. As a young worker I noticed that the agency did not serve many physically challenged individuals. I also noticed that the building was not accessible to those who were handicapped. I shared my observations with the director and gave him a list of what could be done to make the building accessible and the approximate cost of doing so. He responded that the building did not need to be accessible because the agency did not serve any physically challenged individuals. I then retorted that it did not serve the physically challenged because it was not accessible. This became a long-running issue between us, but finally the agency began to take steps to install an elevator and make the building accessible to those who were handicapped. Thus, one form of striving to practice social and economic justice is to recognize existing conditions that may be oppressive or discriminatory and work to remove those impediments, even when it is contrary to agency policy.

The United States came into being as a refuge for people fleeing oppression and discrimination. At the same time, the Puritan tradition emphasized individual responsibility. There is an inevitable conflict between the value of society taking care of its less fortunate members and that of people having to be responsible for their own well-being. Yet, because of social work's dual perspective of enhancing human well-being through individual change as well as community or social change, we are in a special position to help resolve this conflict.

Let me provide a biblical reference to visualize this. Matzah is referred to as the bread of affliction. It is called that because it is a reminder of the slavery that the Israelites experienced in Egypt. Bread was supposedly prepared in haste as the Israelites prepared to leave Egypt, so there was no time for the dough to rise.

The process is replicated today in the preparation of matzah. The formula, a little more scientific now, involves a mixing and baking process that is so specific that there isn't time for atmospheric yeast to enter the dough and cause it to rise. In addition, each piece of matzah is scored with holes to permit any gases in the dough to escape so the matzah will remain flat. Matzah is eaten during the eight days of Passover as a reminder of those times of slavery and as part of the Jewish tradition that is characterized by the phrase "All who are hungry, let them come and eat." The concept of eating matzah as a reminder of slavery and inviting those who are hungry to join in the meal reflect issues of social and economic justice.

Matzah (Bread of Affliction)

1½ cups flour

½ cup water

Mix the flour and water together in a bowl and start a timer for 18 minutes. Mix thoroughly and then cut the dough into 20 pieces. Roll each piece until it's thin. Score the pieces with a metal comb, metal tooth roller, or a fork. Bake in a hot oven, about 550 degrees, until the edges are brown (about 5 minutes). The timer is set because it should not take longer than 18 minutes from the time the water touches the flour till the matzah is placed in the oven. If it takes longer than 18 minutes, then the leavening process will have already begun.

Some people refer to rye bread as poor people's bread. Perhaps it's perceived this way because it doesn't contain some of the ingredients that many breads contain. In addition, it has a base or sour that comes from other breads. In fact, the secret to rye bread comes from its sour. Sour can be easily made by taking a piece of unbaked dough from any other bread, adding water and rye flour to it, and setting it in a cool place for 24 hours to let the dough ferment. The dough may be made more acidic by adding a quartered onion to this mixture. Another way to make a sour is by the following recipe.

Rye Bread Sour

2 oz cake yeast	2½ cups rye flour
1 cup water	¼ onion

Mix the ingredients and place them in a lightly covered container. Let the container sit in a cool place (or refrigerate) for 24 hours. Remove the onion. Yield: approximately 3 cups.

Rye Bread

2½ tbsp salt	1 cup rye flour
2 cups sour	11 cups clear flour (or use
2 cups water	more rye flour and less
½ oz cake yeast or	clear flour for a stronger
2 packages dry yeast	rye taste)

Mix in an electric mixer with a dough hook until the dough is smooth (about 10 minutes). Remove from the mixer and place on a board dusted with rye flour. Let rise about 1 hour. Cut into three equal pieces (each should weigh about 18 ounces). If caraway seeds are desired, place them on the board and blend into the cut pieces of dough. Allow the dough to rise again for 20 minutes. Shape the breads in ovals and place them on a corn meal dusted baking sheet and allow them to rise for about an hour. When they have doubled in size, preheat oven to 450 degrees. It is best to bake the breads with steam in the oven. If you do not have steam in your oven, take a plant mister and mist the inside of the oven for about 3 minutes before adding the breads. Wash the breads with plain water and cut the tops with three or four cuts about 1/4 inch deep. Place them in the oven and bake with steam for 5 minutes (mist the breads with the plant mister after you put them in the oven). Bake for about 20 more minutes.

Critical Thinking Prompts

- What criteria do you use to determine whether the United States is a just society?

- Identify a situation that you felt was socially or economically unjust. What actions did you take in that situation?

- What do you think social workers should do to alleviate conditions contributing to social and economic injustice?

CHAPTER 10

Social Work Values and Ethics

WHAT'S IN THIS CHAPTER:

- Definition of values and ethics and how they relate to social work

- Discussion of confidentiality within social work

- Description of informed consent within social work

- Discussion of self-determination when working with clients

- Discussion of the relationship of technology and social work practice his chapter could very easily have been the first chapter since values and ethics permeate the role and function of all professions and professionals. Values and ethics are so important to our profession that they are the only elements that the Council on Social Work Education states are to be infused throughout the curriculum. *Infusion* is a term that relates to combining two elements to create a new, completely different element.

A cup of tea is the result of infusion. To make a cup of tea, we take two different items, dry tea leaves and boiling water. When we combine the two, we have a new product.

Each of the curricular standards that has been mentioned so far can be related to a standard used by another profession. What makes each standard unique to social work is the infusion of social work values and ethics into that standard. That is, by definition, all professions contain the following elements:

- A cognitive or intellectual component—expertise grounded in a relatively abstract, systematic, and communicative body of theory constantly replenished by discussion and research—transmitted by professional training and higher education
- Authority in society to speak for the needs of the recipient group and members of the profession
- Ethical codes: a normative "collectivity and service orientation" that places client needs above worker interests
- A monopoly to exclusively recruit and educate members, regulate, evaluate, and censure the professional behavior of colleagues
- A professional culture: an organized group performing social functions within the matrix of society that requires socialization to its norms and ethics (Greenwood, as stated in Day, 1997, pp. 48–49)

Social work subscribes to these elements and also has a code of ethics (recently revised) that clarifies those standards that represent the profession. As a social work student, it is important that you become acculturated into the profession by learning about the code of ethics and the values of the profession. In structuring a social work curriculum to address these concerns, the CPS states:

Students must be assisted to develop an awareness of their personal values and to clarify conflicting values and ethical dilemmas. Among the values and principles that must be *infused* [emphasis is mine] throughout every social work curriculum are the following:

Social workers' professional relationships are built on regard for individual worth and dignity and are furthered by mutual participation, acceptance, confidentiality, honesty, and responsible handling of conflict.

Social workers respect people's right to make independent decisions and to participate actively in the helping process.

Social workers are committed to assisting client systems to obtain needed resources.

Social workers strive to make social institutions more humane and responsive to human needs.

Social workers demonstrate respect for and acceptance of the unique characteristics of diverse populations.

Social workers are responsible for their own ethical conduct, the quality of their practice, and seeking continuous growth in the knowledge and skills of their profession. (Council on Social Work Education, 1994, pp. 100, 139)

As you can see from this list, there are a number of aspects that have already been mentioned in earlier chapters of this book. For example, making social institutions more humane relates to the social and economic justice standard and accepting the unique characteristic of diverse populations relates to the cultural diversity standard. But there are a couple of elements from the CPS that I would like to highlight here: confidentiality, informed consent, and a client's right to self-determination.

Confidentiality

Confidentiality means that a social worker "may not disclose information about a client without the client's consent" (Barker, 1995, p. 74). This is important for two reasons. First, it helps to solidify the helping process between the worker and the client. This is accomplished by demonstrating a level of respect between them. The social worker, in maintaining confidentiality, "convey(s) respect and affirm(s) the worth of clients" (Hepworth, Rooney, & Larsen, 1997, p. 78). Second, confidentiality reassures the client that what is being said will be protected. That is, the client gains a sense of comfort by knowing that information that could be embarrassing or damaging will be kept in private by the worker (Sheafor, Horejsi, & Horejsi, 1997, p. 81).

It is important to let the client know that there are degrees of confidentiality, that there are both absolute and relative forms of confidentiality. "Absolute confidentiality refers to a situation when information imparted by the client can never go beyond the social worker" (Sheafor, Horejsi, & Horejsi, 1997, p. 81). Absolute forms of anything are usually difficult to uphold. A more realistic approach to confidentiality is a relative approach. Relative confidentiality means "that the most the social worker can promise is to act responsibly within the profession's *Code of Ethics*, adhere to existing laws, and follow agency policy concerning the handling of client information" (Sheafor, Horejsi, & Horejsi, 1997, p. 81).

Information about a client can be shared if the social worker has permission from the client to share that information.

Informed Consent

When information about a client is requested by others, it is important to obtain written informed consent by the client. This releases you and the agency from liability in disclosing the information (Hepworth, Rooney, & Larsen, 1997, p. 77). Informed consent goes beyond just the release of information, though. Barker (1995) defines it as "the granting of permission by the client to the social worker and agency or other professional person to use specific interventions, including diagnosis, treatment, follow-up, and research. This information must be based on full disclosure of the facts needed to make the decision intelligently. Informed consent must be based on knowledge of the risks and alternatives" (p. 187). Thus, informed consent concerns both the sharing of information and the granting of permission by the client prior to performing an intervention. It is this latter component that leads to the concept of the client's right to self-determination.

Self-Determination

Self-determination is an ethical principle stated in the social work code of ethics that "recognizes the rights and needs of clients to be free to make their own choices and decisions" (Barker, 1995, p. 339; Hepworth, Rooney, & Larsen, 1997, p. 75). Unfortunately, this may be easier said than done. As with confidentiality, the concept is easy to understand but its implementation may not be. The ability to carry out self-determination is, in a large part, related to one's definition of the helping role and the helping process (Hepworth, Rooney, & Larsen, 1997, p. 75). That is, it is important that we understand how we define our role in working with a client and the process that we use in carrying out this process. There are a number of areas where conflict may arise. For example, if one is working within the field of corrections, self-determination may mean that the client would be discharged. However, the system may dictate that the person has to complete the sentence. Or if one is working with children, the minor child may want something that is completely contrary to his or her parent's wishes or may not be in the child's best interest. Therefore, self-determination is important to understand within a context that integrates the individual's needs and interests with those of the larger system.

Social Work's Code of Ethics

Social work values are important and very complex. The profession has worked hard at developing guidelines for the ethical behavior for social workers. The interrelationship between values and practice is reflected by the preamble from the *Code of Ethics* of the National Association of Social Workers (1996). The preamble begins: "The primary mission of the social work profession is to enhance human well-being and help meet the basic human needs of all people" (p. 1). It ends: "Core values, and the principles that flow from them, must be balanced within the context and complexity of the human experience." Since social work relates to the human experience, it is not enough to just have a course on values and ethics—every aspect of our professional behavior should relate to the values and ethics of the profession.

What food comes to mind in thinking about social work values and ethics? It could be something that relates to any of the standards. It could also be something that demonstrates the conscious use of self in order to create a change of state. What comes to my mind is a crème brûlée (a French custard known for its caramelized sugar glaze).

Technology has enhanced our ability to prepare foods in a timely manner. Yet, regardless of the technology, custards and brûlées still involve a consistent level of self in order to be able to gain the proper consistency of the dessert. There is an aspect of art within the process, just like the art within social work.

Crème Brûlée

2 cups whipping cream	2 tbsp sugar
4 large eggs, well beaten	brown sugar

In a double boiler heat the cream until hot (be careful not to boil it). Pour the heated cream into the beaten eggs, making sure to constantly beat while pouring. Once the entire mixture is mixed together, return it to the double boiler and add the sugar. Continue mixing and heating the mixture until the eggs thicken and the custard heavily coats the mixing spoon. Once thick, pour into six custard cups and chill well. After the custard has chilled for at least 8 hours, place the custard cups in a shallow baking pan and surround the cups with ice. Put about a ¼-inch layer of lump-free brown sugar on top of each cup and place the pan under a hot broiler long enough for the sugar to form a crust. Keep the oven door open and turn the pan often to keep the sugar from scorching and to maintain its even caramelizing. Serves 6.

Note: If you do not have a double boiler, you can simulate one by boiling water in a large pot and inserting a smaller pot into the larger pot. The steam from the large pot is what cooks the contents in the small pot.

There are a number of recipes in this text that can be easily adapted to the modern conveniences of our technology. But sometimes, as with crème brûlée, the old methods seem to work best. Recently, I put away the gadgets and returned to basic hand preparations. No longer does the mixer mix my dough, and there is a difference. The mixer did mix the dough more evenly and reduced the amount of time that it took to mix. But hand mixing brings me closer to the finished product. It helps me become more involved in the interaction.

In some respects, hand preparations are like social work. Minuchin (1974), in working with families, talks about the need for the social worker to "enter the family" in order to be able to work toward change. ("Entering the family" is a therapeutic term used to refer to the worker actually becoming part of the family system in order to facilitate the change process.) Technology may help to make our lives easier, but it is important to understand the trade-offs of using the technology and make an informed decision about using or not using it. Technology is part of our value system as Americans, and we should understand how it relates to what we hope to accomplish in the change process.

Critical Thinking Prompts

■ Values are very important in social work practice. What are some of the values you find important?

■ Describe a situation where a relative approach to confidentiality would be appropriate.

- How would you go about getting informed consent from a client?
- Describe what a client's right to self-determination means to you.
- How do you think technology relates to social work practice?

REFERENCES

Barker, R. L. (1995). *The social work dictionary* (3rd ed.). Washington, DC: NASW Press.

Brill, N. I. (1995). *Working with people* (5th ed.). White Plains, NY: Longman.

Carkhuff, R. R., & Anthony, W. A. (1979). *The skills of helping: An introduction to counseling skills.* Amherst, MA: Human Resource Development Press.

Chatterjee, P. (1996). *Approaches to the welfare state.* Washington, DC: NASW Press.

Chess, W. C., & Norlin, J. M. (1991). *Human behavior and the social environment: A social systems model* (2nd ed.). Boston: Allyn & Bacon.

Collins, D., Thomlison, B., & Grinnell, R. M., Jr. (1992). *The social work practicum: A student guide.* Itasca, IL: F. E. Peacock.

Council on Social Work Education. (1994). *Handbook of accreditation standards and procedures* (4th ed.). Alexandria, VA: Author.

Cournoyer, B. (1996). *The social work skills workbook* (2nd ed.). Pacific Grove, CA: Brooks/Cole.

Covey, S. (1989). *The 7 habits of highly effective people: Restoring the character ethic.* New York: Simon & Schuster.

Day, P. I. (1997). *A new history of social welfare* (2nd ed.). Boston: Allyn & Bacon.

Devore, W., & Schlesinger, E. G. (1991). *Ethnic-sensitive social work practice* (3rd ed.). New York: Macmillan.

Doweiko, H. E. (1996). *Concepts of chemical dependency* (3rd ed.). Pacific Grove, CA: Brooks/Cole.

DuBois, B., & Miley, K. K. (1996). *Social work: An empowering profession* (2nd ed.). Boston: Allyn & Bacon.

Dye, T. R. (1987). *Understanding public policy* (6th ed.). Englewood Cliffs, NJ: Prentice- Hall.

Friedman, B. D. (1993). *No place like home: A study of two homeless shelters.* Ann Arbor, MI: UMI Dissertation Services.

Friedman, B. D. (1997). Systems theory. In J. R. Brandell (Ed.), *Theory and practice in clinical social work* (pp. 3–17). New York: Free Press.

Friedman, B. D. (1998). *The research tool kit: Putting it all together.* Pacific Grove, CA: Brooks/Cole.

Friedman, B. D., & Levine-Holdowsky, M. (1997). Overcoming barriers to homeless delivery services: A community response. *Journal of Social Distress and the Homeless, 6* (1): 13–28.

Friedman, B. D., & Neuman, K. M. (1997, October). Learning plans: A tool for forging allegiances in social work. Paper presented at the annual conference of the BPD, Philadelphia, PA.

Furr, L. A. (1997). *Exploring human behavior and the social environment.* Boston: Allyn & Bacon.

Germain, C. B. (1991). *Human behavior in the social environment: An ecological view.* New York: Columbia University Press.

Ginsberg, L. H. (1998). *Careers in social work.* Boston: Allyn & Bacon.

Hepworth, D. H., Rooney, R. H., & Larsen, J. A. (1997). *Direct social work practice: Theory and skills* (5th ed.). Pacific Grove, CA: Brooks/Cole.

Hoffman, K. S., & Sallee, A. L. (1994). *Social work practice: Bridges to change.* Boston: Allyn & Bacon.

Iglehart, A. P., & Becerra, R. M. (1995). *Social services and the ethnic community.* Boston: Allyn & Bacon.

Karger, H. J., & Stoesz, D. (1998). *American social welfare policy: A pluralist approach* (3rd ed.). New York: Addison-Wesley Longman.

Marlowe, C. (1998). *Research methods for generalist social work* (2nd ed.). Pacific Grove, CA: Brooks/Cole.

Maslow, A. H. (1970). *Motivation and personality* (2nd ed.). New York: Harper & Row.

McMahon, M. O. (1994). *Advanced generalist practice: With an international perspective.* Englewood Cliffs, NJ: Prentice-Hall.

Miley, K. K., O'Melia, M., & DuBois, B. L. (1998). *Generalist social work practice: An empowerment approach* (2nd ed.). Boston: Allyn & Bacon.

Minuchin, S. (1974). *Families & family therapy.* Cambridge, MA: Harvard University Press.

Morales, A. T., & Sheafor, B. W. (1998). *Social work: A profession of many faces* (8th ed.). Boston: Allyn & Bacon.

National Association of Social Workers (NASW). (1996). *Code of ethics.* Washington, DC: Author.

Neuman, K. M., & Friedman, B. D. (1997). Process recording: Fine-tuning an old instrument. *Journal of Social Work Education, 33* (2): 237–243.

Popple, P. R., & Leighninger, L. (1996). *Social work, social welfare, and American society* (3rd ed.). Boston: Allyn & Bacon.

Reid, W. J., Rodwell, M. K., & Bricout, J. (1997). Is neo-positivism a suitable epistemological framework for HBSE courses? In M. Bloom & W. C. Klein (Eds.), *Controversial issues in human behavior in the social environment* (pp. 2–15). Boston: Allyn & Bacon.

Royse, D., Dhooper, S. S., & Rompf, E. L. (1993). *Field instruction: A guide for social work students.* White Plains, NY: Longman.

Schorr, A. L. (1986). *Common decency: Domestic policies after Reagan.* New Haven, CT: Yale University Press.

Sheafor, B. W., Horejsi, C. R., & Horejsi, G. A. (1997). *Techniques and guidelines for social work practice* (4th ed.). Boston: Allyn & Bacon.

Specht, H., & Courtney, M. E. (1994). *Unfaithful angels: How social work has abandoned its mission.* New York: Free Press.

Stone, S., & Stone, M. (1988). *The brilliant bean.* Toronto, Canada: Bantam Books.

Thomlinson, B., Collins, D., & Grinnell, R. M., Jr. (1996). *The social work practicum: An access guide.* Itasca, IL: F. E. Peacock.

RECIPE INDEX

SUBJECT INDEX

TO THE OWNER OF THIS BOOK:

I hope that you have found *The Ecological Perspectives Cookbook: Recipes for Social Workers* useful. So that this book can be improved in a future edition, would you take the time to complete this sheet and return it? Thank you.

School and address: _____

Department: _____

Instructor's name: _____

1. What I like most about this book is: _____

_____

_____

2. What I like least about this book is: _____

_____

_____

3. My general reaction to this book is: _____

_____

4. The name of the course in which I used this book is: _____

_____

5. Were all of the chapters of the book assigned for you to read?

Yes_____ No_____

If not, which ones weren't? _____

6. On a separate sheet of paper, please write specific suggestions for improving this book and anything else you'd care to share about your experience in using the book.

Optional:

Your name: _____ Date: _____

May Brooks/Cole quote you, either in promotion for *The Ecological Perspectives Cookbook: Recipes for Social Workers*, or in future publishing ventures?

Yes: _____ No: _____

Sincerely,

Bruce D. Friedman